The Executive Function Playbook

The Executive Function Playbook

BUILDING INDEPENDENCE IN KIDS WITH ADHD

MICHAEL McLEOD

JB JOSSEY-BASS
A Wiley Brand

Copyright © 2026 by John Wiley & Sons, Inc. All rights reserved, including rights for text and data mining and training of artificial intelligence technologies or similar technologies.

Published by John Wiley & Sons, Inc., Hoboken, New Jersey.

No part of this publication may be reproduced, stored in a retrieval system, or transmitted in any form or by any means, electronic, mechanical, photocopying, recording, scanning, or otherwise, except as permitted under Section 107 or 108 of the 1976 United States Copyright Act, without either the prior written permission of the Publisher, or authorization through payment of the appropriate per-copy fee to the Copyright Clearance Center, Inc., 222 Rosewood Drive, Danvers, MA 01923, (978) 750-8400, fax (978) 750-4470, or on the web at www.copyright.com. Requests to the Publisher for permission should be addressed to the Permissions Department, John Wiley & Sons, Inc., 111 River Street, Hoboken, NJ 07030, (201) 748-6011, fax (201) 748-6008, or online at http://www.wiley.com/go/permission.

The manufacturer's authorized representative according to the EU General Product Safety Regulation is Wiley-VCH GmbH, Boschstr. 12, 69469 Weinheim, Germany, • e-mail: Product_Safety@wiley.com.

Trademarks: Wiley and the Wiley logo are trademarks or registered trademarks of John Wiley & Sons, Inc. and/or its affiliates in the United States and other countries and may not be used without written permission. All other trademarks are the property of their respective owners. John Wiley & Sons, Inc. is not associated with any product or vendor mentioned in this book.

Limit of Liability/Disclaimer of Warranty: While the publisher and author have used their best efforts in preparing this book, they make no representations or warranties with respect to the accuracy or completeness of the contents of this book and specifically disclaim any implied warranties of merchantability or fitness for a particular purpose. No warranty may be created or extended by sales representatives or written sales materials. The advice and strategies contained herein may not be suitable for your situation. You should consult with a professional where appropriate. Further, readers should be aware that websites listed in this work may have changed or disappeared between when this work was written and when it is read. Neither the publisher nor authors shall be liable for any loss of profit or any other commercial damages, including but not limited to special, incidental, consequential, or other damages.

For general information on our other products and services or for technical support, please contact our Customer Care Department within the United States at (800) 762-2974, outside the United States at (317) 572-3993 or fax (317) 572-4002.

Wiley also publishes its books in a variety of electronic formats. Some content that appears in print may not be available in electronic formats. For more information about Wiley products, visit our web site at www.wiley.com.

Library of Congress Cataloging-in-Publication Data:

Names: McLeod, Michael (Executive function coach) author
Title: The executive function playbook : building independence in kids with
   ADHD / Michael McLeod.
Description: Hoboken, New Jersey : Jossey-Bass, [2026] | Includes
   bibliographical references and index.
Identifiers: LCCN 2025028286 (print) | LCCN 2025028287 (ebook) | ISBN
   9781394309153 paperback | ISBN 9781394309177 adobe pdf | ISBN
   9781394309160 epub
Subjects: LCSH: Attention-deficit hyperactivity disorder in adolescence |
   Autonomy in youth | Parents of children with attention-deficit
   hyperactivity disorder
Classification: LCC RJ506.H9 M4245 2026 (print) | LCC RJ506.H9 (ebook)
LC record available at https://lccn.loc.gov/2025028286
LC ebook record available at https://lccn.loc.gov/2025028287

Cover Design: Wiley
Cover Image: © TWINS DESIGN STUDIO/stock.adobe.com (modified by Wiley)
Author Photo: © Michael McLeod

Contents

Foreword by Dr. Lawrence Brown
of Children's Hospital of Philadelphia   vii

Chapter 1   Your New Parenting Playbook   1

Chapter 2   The Foundation I: Nonverbal Working Memory and Visual Imagery   17

Chapter 3   The Foundation II: Verbal Working Memory and Self-Talk   27

Part I   Self-Awareness   41

Chapter 4   The First Pillar   43

Chapter 5   The Playbook on Self-Awareness   55

Part II   Self-Regulation   69

Chapter 6   The Second Pillar: What You Deal with Most Often   71

Chapter 7   The Playbook on Self-Regulation   83

Part III	Self-Motivation	103
Chapter 8	The Third Pillar: Everything Is Nonpreferred	105
Chapter 9	The Playbook on Self-Motivation	117
Part IV	Self-Evaluation	137
Chapter 10	The Final Pillar: Developing True Independence	139
Chapter 11	The Playbook on Self-Evaluation	147
Chapter 12	ADHD Hope	163
Acknowledgments		183
References		185
Index		201

Foreword by Dr. Lawrence Brown of Children's Hospital of Philadelphia

ADHD is constantly in the news, but how can it be possible? One day there are headlines about an explosion of children (and adults) with ADHD; the next day a new study reports that ADHD is markedly over-diagnosed. Actually, both are true, since it is a developmental neuropsychiatric disorder that overlaps with normal neurodiversity, which has only behavioral criteria, and that is subject to many confounding variables from age to gender to comorbidities like oppositionality and mood. ADHD can coexist with, be exacerbated by, or even be present as the first symptom of illness from infection to metabolic disease, genetic syndrome, or cancer. Environmental toxins like lead poisoning or social circumstances like food insecurity and emotional deprivation can also lead to a condition that fulfills current criteria for ADHD. Similarly, primary sleep disorders can lead to daytime fatigue, inattentiveness, and learning challenges that mimic or worsen underlying ADHD. There is no scientific doubt that what we call ADHD by current criteria is real, has always been present in the population, and is vulnerable to the differing criteria by which it is defined. Indeed, whenever social scientists have used the same set of criteria, ADHD is present to a similar degree around the world. Those findings can be underestimated by governments that prefer to explain away symptoms (e.g., by labeling the cardinal signs as lack of motivation) or overestimated (e.g., in communities where academic underachievement is blamed on ADHD).

The very term *attention deficit hyperactivity disorder* is a product of evolution over the past 50 years. When I was in medical school in the early 1970s, what we now call ADHD was referred to as *minimal brain dysfunction* or *minimal cerebral dysfunction.*

The formal name ADHD was first invented in 1980. It was only in the third edition of the *Diagnostic and Statistical Manual of Mental Disorders (DSM III)* that the American Psychiatric Association redefined the core deficits we know as ADHD as either inattentiveness and/or hyperactivity. This led to a marked explosion of the disorder now that many individuals without externalizing behavior—polite, quiet, dreamy, low-achieving—were first recognized. A major result of this change was the demographic shift that suddenly emphasized the diagnosis in females who had previously been dramatically underrepresented. It was in 1987 that DSM-IIIR changed the nomenclature to ADHD, and the name has remained in subsequent editions. In the current DSM-5, there are three ADHD presentations. Approximately one-third of people with ADHD have the predominantly inattentive presentation, meaning that they do not have the hyperactive or overactive behavior components of the combined presentation.

Over the past five decades, much of the focus in the medical community has been on a search for safer and more effective drugs to improve upon or replace the standard treatment with immediate release stimulants including methylphenidate and dextroamphetamine. While these preparations are clearly effective in reducing symptoms, they come with a host of potential negatives from wide swings in energy and focus to appetite suppression, growth inhibition, and the potential for dangerous misuse like diversion and abuse. But since they treated symptoms so well, physicians learned to minimize the downsides and often embraced new delivery symptoms, such as time-delayed preparations that smoothed out the ping-pong behavior and delivered peak concentrations at times when it was needed, or even capsules taken at bedtime (despite the known stimulating effects) that are not absorbed into the blood stream for 8 or more hours so that the individual has the benefit of awakening effectively medicated. The latter has proven to be a lifesaver for those who are so disorganized or combative in the morning that they are late for school or start the day with a negative mood or already punished.

Specialists, both physicians and psychologists, have always known that medication, while often essential for optimal outcome, is not the whole story and should never be the first approach. A full medical evaluation should always be the first step. This can identify whether the concerns are even developmentally appropriate—for example, no four-year-old should be expected to sit quietly for an hour or be criticized for not routinely taking turns with peers. A pediatrician will screen for ADHD mimics such as anemia, lead poisoning, poor vision or hearing, signs of underlying medical disorders or even social consequences from food insecurity to a lack of enriched environment. Correcting misinformation about developmental expectations or addressing treatable issues can reassure or minimize symptoms to the point that what was troubling behavior is now within the broad range of normal variability and no longer requires intervention or fits criteria for a disorder. Even if there are clear symptoms of ADHD without confounding condition, the first step should never be a prescription but rather a nonpharmacologic approach that provides parental education, guidance, and support as well as a child-oriented program that offers age and developmentally appropriate management that can lead to positivity and resilience with academic, social, and behavioral success. This is especially important for preschool and early elementary school–aged children.

The focus of this book is educational and practical. It offers a primer on the variations of behavior that comprise ADHD and emphasizes the overarching theme of a neurodevelopmental delay in executive function that underlies those behaviors. There are detailed descriptions of the manifold ways that delay affects daily life at home, school, and play. Beyond outlining the broad effects on the individual and their environment, this book outlines practical solutions with great skill and sensitivity, never blaming the child or the family.

Nowhere in the defining characteristics of ADHD is there mention of executive function. Mr. McLeod builds a comprehensive case for failure of executive function as the missing link. His description of the four pillars of executive function is the key to understanding and learning to function with ADHD: Self-Awareness, Self-Motivation, Self-Regulation, and Self-Evaluation. Even as a young child, it can be a disaster if one is unable to self-monitor. Without self-awareness one cannot recognize an inappropriate, dangerous, or unsuccessful situation. Especially in younger children this can lead to impulsive, aggressive, or disruptive "externalizing" behavior symptoms, failure to take turns, tantrums, or inability to learn from mistakes. In some children it can also lead to "internalizing" symptoms such as withdrawal into dreaminess, passivity, anxiety, or depression. Since girls are less likely to act out, the recognition of the inattentive type of ADHD has significantly reduced the male predominance of ADHD. The second pillar is self-regulation, which redefines ADHD. Mr. McLeod makes the case that hyperactivity is difficulty in self-regulating one's body, while inattentiveness is the inability to self-regulate one's thoughts. Unfortunately, whether it is lashing out in frustration at friends or failing to limit video games in order to complete school assignments, failure to self-regulate can lead to a vicious cycle of self-sabotage: anger, getting "stupid," and losing the ability to think rationally.

Equally important is the concept of self-motivation that allows an individual to accept responsibilities and social demands that compete with more compelling interests. The ability to play video games for hours does not preclude ADHD—rather, it is the inability to carry out essential, but nonpreferred, activities that is the hallmark of the executive function weakness of ADHD. Such challenges can play out as failing to get ready for school, finding excuses to delay completing chores, or even refusing to reach out to friends or unwillingness to leave their safety of home and participate in activities like sports or playdates. Self-awareness and self-motivation are necessary but insufficient without the ability to self-evaluate. Otherwise, as Mr. McLeod notes it is Groundhog Day, and the failures and frustrations are repeated.

Fortunately, this book does not just lay out the problem; it provides clear and concrete solutions grounded in the latest neuroscience and forceful in its clinically based successes to help families to push back on widely accepted norms like allowing screen time for decompress after a challenging day at school or the increasing availability of school-provided computers. Some of the advice is even more counterintuitive than restricting or eliminating screen time. For example, it is surprising, but extremely sobering, to learn that school accommodations like individualized education plans and 504 plans can be double-edged swords that can provide support but complicate parent–child relationships by making parents responsible for the child's unacceptable school behavior or academic failure. Mr. McLeod provides detailed description of specific strategies on how to shift the burden from parents to the child's acceptance of increased accountability and consequences and to the school to provide structured expectations with opportunities for the skill-building that fosters independence. He also has strong advice for parents; while recognizing the unconditional love they have for their child with ADHD, he insists that they recognize that their neurodiverse child requires different home support to become self-motivated and self-responsible. Again, proven advice is doled out with specificity and practicality.

So, for everyone involved with children and adolescents with ADHD—parents, teachers, counselors, school administrators, doctors, and therapists—this is a welcome handbook that will guide youth affected with ADHD to resilience, independence, and success in life.

CHAPTER 1

Your New Parenting Playbook

The strong desire to create what I always needed.
Something that could have helped me.
Something that will help others to avoid what I went through, and what I continue to experience every day.

That has always been my goal, my dream, my purpose.

When I was growing up, many days were a struggle, especially in high school when everyone around me gained a level of maturity and social functioning that I simply didn't have yet. I never quite fit in and was never fully accepted. The lack of relationships and experiences takes a toll on you. It results in not having a strong social network and not having enough varied experiences, further inhibiting the development of the exact skills I needed.

I graduated high school in 2005, a time when ADHD was not fully understood or properly cared for. Did students even have individual education plans (IEPs) back then? If a child received any type of therapy after school, that was a very big deal. No one spoke about it, though; it was not openly discussed.

There were many things I could have done differently as a child and teen to improve my situation, but I didn't. Overall, my lack of self-awareness was debilitating. But that isn't an excuse. This isn't going to be a story about being a victim. Blaming my brain, the school system, the people around me—that gets me nowhere. Blaming doesn't get anyone anywhere.

My entire plan in life was to be a teacher so I could work directly with youth, inspire them, and give them the tools I needed as a child. It wasn't until I was a counselor at a residential treatment facility in Yonkers, New York, that I learned about speech–language pathology. I was instantly hooked. Instead of teaching students about math, science, and history—information they would honestly rarely use in their lives—I could work on skills that were directly correlated to quality of life. Skills that actually help because they improve self-worth, self-confidence, friendships, and life success. Skills that made kids and teens feel good about themselves. I immediately went back to college for my second bachelor's degree, and then eventually, in 2015, I graduated with my master's in speech–language pathology from Lehman College in New York City.

A major theme of this book is going to be discussing things that are widely misunderstood. Speech–language pathology (SLP) is one of them. Most people hear about speech therapy, and they think it's just professionals that deal with articulation, pronunciation, the "s" sound, the "r" sound, or stuttering. Those things are an incredibly small fraction of the scope of practice of an SLP.

First, speech and language are two different things. Speech is what most people think of—the ability to be understood by a listener when you speak. Language is different. Language is expressive: it's the words, syntax, and morphology that you use to express yourself. It is also receptive—the ability to comprehend what you hear and develop a coherent and appropriate response. Language is also the social-pragmatic ability to converse with others so you can have successful social dialogues to make friends and keep them over time.

It was during my time as an SLP that I had the privilege of partnering with a national organization known as The Focus Foundation, based in Annapolis, Maryland, that specializes in chromosomal disorders. Initially, I was able to work with this group through another SLP who was supervising me because she was a motor speech specialist, and many of these children presented with apraxia of speech, which is a disorder that can significantly affect your intelligibility. It turned out that, along with apraxia, many of them also presented with ADHD and significant delays in their executive function system. I quickly learned that there was very little out there to help them with their ADHD symptoms. Counseling and talk therapy weren't working. I needed to create something.

I found myself with the perfect opportunity. I had the privilege to work side-by-side with some of the most amazing doctors and specialists in the entire country. I soaked up every single bit of information I could, and I loved every minute of it. From this opportunity, I decided to devote my entire life to learn everything I could about ADHD and executive functioning. I dedicated my time, finances, and energy toward learning from incredible professionals: Dr. Russell Barkley, Dr. George McCloskey, Dr. Peg Dawson, Sarah Ward, and many more. I quickly learned that the field of ADHD is incredibly small. This amazed me, as it is one of the most common psychiatric disorders, affecting 1 in every 9 children (Danielson et al. 2024) and 1 in every 22 adults (Kessler et al. 2006).

Another thing I quickly noticed was that there was such a major gap between what these incredible specialists were saying about ADHD and what everyone else seemed to believe. The specialists described it as something very serious—something that significantly affects parts of the brain that are crucial to life success. Meanwhile, everyone else discussed ADHD as a "gift" that would only affect them in school. With some movement breaks and a fidget spinner, a child with ADHD would be just fine.

Soon, it was clear to me that ADHD was widely misunderstood by the general public, and this massive misunderstanding was negatively impacting kids because they were receiving outdated treatments that were not supported by the American Academy of Pediatrics. These parents were spending a lot of time and money on therapy for their children and seeing absolutely zero progress. Even worse, they tended to have no idea what was even happening in the sessions with the therapist. There was no communication at all. No parent coaching, no homework.

I wholeheartedly disagreed with most of what I learned in graduate school, what I saw while working in the schools, and how most private practices ran. All we ever did was push square pegs into round holes. We were trying to make kids into mini-adults. We pathologized them so much and tried to push them into an adult model of education and therapy, which made absolutely no sense to them at all. Everything was so data-driven and so focused on rigid goals. Why no focus on relationships? What about giving them experiences instead of worksheets or just sitting and talking? Why were parents so rarely involved?

It was obvious to me that there had to be a better way.

This is why I started GrowNOW. GrowNOW is my heart and my life's mission statement: to give kids, teens, and youth the strength to persevere through anything. To always be their own unique self—but to have an internal system of checks and balances to ensure they are always focusing on learning from the past and visualizing the future so they can make healthy and positive choices for a lifetime and always engaging in positive and motivating internal speech. Whether at school, at home, or socially, they can always be confident, they can push past any mistakes and move forward. Keep moving forward—toward their dreams and to becoming their best selves.

With GrowNOW, I wanted to make sure our clinics were different from everything else out there. I wanted to implement a coaching model that kids and teens who have already been through the gamut of failed therapies and counseling could go to and say, "Wow, this is different. I like this, I want to keep doing this, I feel good about myself here." And this is exactly what I created.

Today, GrowNOW serves families all across America and internationally. We have a team of highly trained coaches providing unique and intensive parent coaching. We do virtual sessions that are nothing like COVID-19 virtual school, and we also have multiple locations across the country, with plans to open several more. I have had the privilege of traveling across the globe to train various school districts and professionals to ensure they have the tools to help not only their ADHD students but every single student they ever interact with.

As an individual with ADHD, this is what I have chosen to devote my life to. I have struggled my entire life with never feeling fully accepted, unable to fit in and do what's right. I can't go back in time to change my childhood and use the knowledge I have now to better inform myself. All I can do is pass along my lessons, follow the research, and tell the hard truths.

After working with thousands of families and consulting with hundreds of schools throughout my career, I've seen firsthand just how much ADHD youth, their families, and their teachers are struggling. Parents especially are feeling helpless. Raising an ADHD child is a daily grind.

As a parent, you are your child's (and probably your entire family's) prefrontal cortex. It's exhausting. Without you, the house would be chaos. Nothing would get done. Nobody would get to school or appointments on time. Homework would never be finished. This is not discussed enough—how parenting an ADHD child is just as stressful as raising a child with other serious disorders (Martin et al. 2019). This is because ADHD is serious—a brain disorder that is highly correlated to serious things.

I'm sorry, but it isn't a gift—no matter how many Instagram and TikTok videos tell you it is. ADHD is highly correlated with substance abuse, job loss, divorce, inability to live alone, automobile accidents, and early death. Fun, silly, happy videos with hundreds of thousands of likes and shares by influencers with millions of followers will tell you how quirky and cool it is to have ADHD. This is not accurate. ADHD has become a cool "trend," partly because of how invisible it is. With the rise of smart computers in our pockets and social media, we now live in a world of pseudoscience where feelings trump facts. There may be more misinformation on ADHD on social media than any other neurobiological disorder.

It's time we clear up the misconceptions, erase the pseudoscience and "trendy" information from our minds, and focus on facts instead of feelings.

So many parents and teachers are still completely lost when it comes to ADHD. Each day they are stuck with the same questions: How do I help? Where do I send my child in the little free time I have? Where do I allocate my funds to help them? What works in the classroom? Why does homework have to be such a huge fight every single day? Why does my child have no friends and never go anywhere after school? Why does my child have no interest in anything besides screens?

At the end of the day, parents and teachers need answers. They need real, practical strategies that are going to bring about real growth and change in the natural environment—not just within a therapy session.

Teachers with ADHD students are baffled about how to properly help.

Parents with ADHD children are burnt out.

Kids and teens with ADHD are feeling broken. They just want to do the right thing, fit in, and end the nonsense and daily fights.

We need to end this very serious youth mental health crisis.

We need ADHD hope.

This book isn't about me or GrowNOW—this is about ADHD hope. Helping teachers, parents, and ADHD kids themselves see that their goals can be achieved and all their dreams can be realized.

Kids and teens with ADHD do not come with an instruction manual. Consider this book your straightforward, no-nonsense playbook. My goal here is to be as brutally honest as possible. What's real, what isn't. What works, what doesn't. This book will discuss research and facts that, many times, will be hard to hear, because that's what ADHD is—hard. It makes life more difficult. It makes parenting more difficult. How do I ensure my child or teen has the highest possible quality of life? Follow the playbook.

I want this book to be a "one-stop shop" for all individuals who come in contact with youth with ADHD: parents, teachers, therapists, counselors, principals, directors, and superintendents. This is going to be about knowledge, acceptance, understanding, passion, and truth—a playbook for success.

ADHD 101

ADHD affects approximately 5–7% of children globally (Polanczyk et al. 2007; Thomas et al. 2015). In the United States, an estimated 9.4% of children ages 2–17 have been diagnosed with ADHD (Danielson et al. 2018). That's around six million children in total in the United States alone. It's quite possibly the most common yet most misunderstood neurological condition.

Thankfully, emerging research is helping us to dispel many of those long-held myths and misconceptions.

At one time, the large majority of children receiving an ADHD diagnosis were boys. This led to a belief that ADHD is uncommon in girls. But what we're seeing now is that boys are more likely to have the hyperactive subtype of ADHD, which tends to include more externalized, disruptive behaviors and is therefore more likely to be noticed as problematic by teachers and parents. Girls, on the other hand, are more likely to have the inattentive type (Biederman et al. 2002), which usually involves fewer externally disruptive behaviors. This can lead to underdiagnosis. In childhood, girls are still diagnosed less often than boys, at a ratio of 1:3 (Barkley 2005).

ADHD was once regarded as a disorder that only affected children. But today, as awareness increases, many people are first receiving a diagnosis as adults (Montejano et al. 2011). We now know that, far from being limited to childhood, ADHD can have wide-ranging impacts all throughout a person's life. ADHD affects 2–7% of adults globally (Song et al. 2021). Around 4.4% of US adults are estimated to have ADHD (Kessler et al. 2006), though many remain undiagnosed.

Despite what is commonly believed, ADHD isn't just a set of behaviors or bad habits. MRI scans have shown structural and functional differences in ADHD brains, particularly in the prefrontal cortex, which is involved in decision-making, attention, and impulse control (Arnsten 2009).

Most of what people do know about ADHD relates to how kids and teens are affected academically. Without a doubt, ADHD has a huge impact on education: Children and adolescents with ADHD are more likely to receive low grades and poor test scores (Kent et al. 2011). Up to 33% of students with ADHD may fail to complete high school, compared to 10–15% of students without ADHD (Barbaresi et al. 2007; Breslau et al. 2011). People with ADHD are significantly less likely to graduate from college, with some studies indicating that only 5–10% of symptomatic individuals complete a degree (Hechtman et al. 2016).

But many aspects of life outside of school are also affected by the disorder. People of any age with ADHD often struggle to regulate their emotions, which can lead to mood swings, outbursts, and difficulty calming down once they're upset. They may have a hard time recognizing and following social cues. Inattentiveness can hinder meaningful communication, and impulsivity makes it difficult to follow through with plans. With all of these emotional and interpersonal challenges to contend with, people with ADHD can find it extremely hard to create and maintain healthy relationships. Individuals with ADHD often report feeling misunderstood by peers (Michielsen et al. 2018), which only worsens their loneliness and anxiety.

It's well-documented that ADHD is associated with a higher likelihood of engaging in impulsive or risky behaviors, which includes those that can result in legal consequences. For example, adolescents and adults with ADHD are more likely to be arrested for traffic violations, reckless driving (Barkley and Cox 2007), or substance use-related offenses (Mohr-Jensen and Steinhausen 2016). We see this reflected in the demographics of our prisons. The prevalence of ADHD is much higher there than in the general population: 30% of youth and 26% of adults in prison have ADHD (Young et al. 2015).

Teenagers and adults with untreated ADHD are more likely to abuse alcohol, nicotine, and other drugs as a way of coping with impulsivity, emotional dysregulation, and stress. The unfortunate reality is that people with ADHD are twice as likely to develop a substance use disorder compared to those without ADHD (Biederman et al. 1995).

Symptoms like impulsivity, inattention, and time management issues can lead to poor work performance, interpersonal conflicts, and missed deadlines. As a result, adults with ADHD are more likely to experience frequent job changes, job loss, or underemployment (Barkley et al. 2008). Individuals with ADHD earn, on average, about 17% less than their non-ADHD counterparts (Jangmo et al. 2021). Over the years, that adds up: ADHD can cost individuals over $1 million in lost wages during the course of their lifetime (Pelham et al. 2020).

I mentioned how much I've seen families struggle to help kids with ADHD. Raising a child with a serious disorder is not easy for anyone, but it can be especially difficult for parents who are disproportionately likely to have ADHD themselves. ADHD is highly heritable. Over 75% of ADHD cases are linked to genetic factors (Faraone et al. 2005). When children and their parents both have ADHD, the combination can create an even more challenging environment at home.

The risks of ADHD encompass every aspect of life, including life expectancy. A Danish study found that people with ADHD are twice as likely to die prematurely compared to the general population (Faraone 2015). This may be due to accidents, substance abuse, risky behaviors, or comorbid conditions like depression. Tragically, adolescents and adults with ADHD have a suicide attempt rate that is about five times higher than the non-ADHD population (Fuller-Thomson et al. 2020).

I'm sharing this because I want you to understand the reality of an ADHD diagnosis. I want to be clear about what's at stake when we talk about youth with ADHD.

But what I don't want is to scare you. Like I said, this is meant to be a book about hope. There's good news: early intervention can greatly improve outcomes, both academically (DuPaul et al. 2015) and socially (DuPaul et al. 2018), for children with ADHD. Executive function skills can be trained and attained. They can gain these skills.

Today, we know more about ADHD than any time in history. With all of this knowledge, we can provide more effective interventions than ever before.

The Four Pillars

If you heard the name "attention-deficit hyperactivity disorder" for the first time, what would it make you think of?

Kids who are extra hyper? Kids who can't sit still? "Ants in their pants"? Kids who need more discipline? Kids who eat too much sugar? Kids with "bad" parents?

Nonsense. And it is exactly these massive misconceptions about ADHD that have given everyone the idea that "maybe I have ADHD too" and "everyone is a little ADHD." This is also one of the ways ADHD has become so trendy on social media. "I'm ADHD! I'm so wacky; I just drive my spouse crazy!" "I'm ADHD; I had to go to the same store today five times because I kept forgetting things." "I'm ADHD; I pick up a brand-new interest every day!"

These terrible misconceptions and stereotypes are exactly the reason why kids and teens with ADHD get labeled as "lazy" and "disinterested." This is also a main reason for parent-blaming. "Oh, that kid is so hyper, he needs more discipline!" "His parents must always let him do what he wants, so when he's at school or in public, he has no boundaries."

The pioneers and leaders in this field agree, ADHD is a terrible name for ADHD.

(We no longer use the term "ADD." If you are working with someone who still uses this term, there is a good chance they are quite behind in their ADHD practices.)

One of the most common things I hear from parents is, "My child has ADHD, and I also think he struggles with executive functions." It is time that we all fully understand this: there is no distinction. They are one and the same. ADHD is a developmental disorder of the executive function system.

Over the first 30 years of life, our brain grows and develops. The direction it grows is from back, behind your ears, to front. This means the prefrontal cortex, the area of the brain right behind the forehead, is the last to develop, and it is not fully developed in some people until around 30 years old (O'Rourke et al. 2020). The prefrontal cortex is the part of the brain responsible for executive functioning. In individuals with ADHD, there will be a developmental delay in this region. This delay is typically 20–45% behind their same-age peers, depending on severity (Barkley 2023). For example, if an individual is 10 years of age, but they have ADHD, their executive function system and maturity may be that of a five- to seven-year-old. Dr. Russell Barkley refers to this as the "executive age."

This is important for parents to understand. When you fully comprehend and accept that your child has a significant delay in self-regulation and overall maturity, their behaviors start to make a lot more sense. When their behaviors start to make more sense, you have a greater ability to stay calm and deal with them appropriately.

To better understand what ADHD is, we have to first understand executive functions. Just like ADHD, executive functions are wildly misunderstood. Still to this day, when most people hear the term "executive functions," the first two things they think of are time management and organization. Messy backpacks, papers all over the place, messy lockers, messy bedrooms, and an inability to use or follow a calendar or an agenda. This idea in no way encapsulates what executive functions truly are, or how unbelievably important they are.

Executive functions are the greatest predictor of success we have for human beings. Strong executive functions indicate an individual has a great chance to graduate, move out of their parents' house, live on their own, get a job, keep a job, make friends, keep friends, pay the bills on time, stay relatively healthy, and live a positive and productive life (Low et al. 2021). So, executive functions must be so much more than just time management and organization, right?

Yes—so much more.

Using the GrowNOW model of executive function, I like to break down these skills into what I call the "Four Pillars." They are: self-awareness, self-regulation, self-motivation, and self-evaluation.

The Four Pillars of executive functioning help us to define this crucial set of skills so we can better help our youth in need. For decades, we looked at ADHD as solely an external, behavior-based disorder. Knowing what we now know about it, it is heartbreaking how we treated this disorder for so long. Schools pushed ADHD kids into "executive function classes" that just taught them how to use an agenda book and keep notes for themselves, not realizing this would never happen unless they were specially told to do it by a teacher. They taught them how to clean their backpacks and organize papers in their folders, which only kept them more prompt dependent on adults. The backpacks stayed messy long after they graduated from these classes.

Families dealt with extreme behaviors in the home after being told their child's ADHD was just about attention and getting work done at school. This explanation left them at a loss as they struggled to understand what they were seeing: "Why does my child yell so much? Why is he always so angry? Why is she always attacking her siblings? Why do they never leave their room? This has to be more than just ADHD!"

Now we know that it is this internal set of skills that is lacking and needs to be developed over time. No more focus on time management and organization, no more outdated beliefs that ADHD is just an issue of keeping up with schoolwork. Nothing is going to get better without the Four Pillars.

The Four Pillars give us a behind-the-scenes view of what these ADHD kids and teens are facing on a daily basis. The constant struggle that makes an already difficult life even more stressful and anxiety-producing. Every day, they're dealing with the same issues, the same fights, the same failures.

These pillars help us to understand the behaviors that we are seeing externally:

(1) **Lack of *self-awareness*:** A child or teen who does not recognize that they are alienating themselves from peers by making offensive jokes or repeating the same jokes over and over. This is a lack of an ability to self-advocate or know what is best for them due to the inability to sense their own strengths and needs.

(2) **Lack of *self-regulation*:** A child or teen who consistently responds with anger, frustration, and aggression toward parents when asked to do a task.

(3) **Lack of *self-motivation:*** A child or teen who does whatever they can to stay within their comfort zones of screens, video games, YouTube, and smartphones and refuses to participate or exhibits negative behaviors when presented with new and novel experiences.

(4) **Lack of *self-evaluation:*** A child or teen who performs the same negative or hurtful act consistently, even after experiencing consequences or seeing the harmful effects to themselves or others.

Now that we have the Four Pillars, we have the inside information on exactly what these kids need. We are no longer guessing, and we are no longer focused solely on inattention and hyperactivity. We see what's lacking, so we can strengthen it, just like any other muscle in the body.

The prefrontal cortex is the last part of the brain to develop, and it is also the most malleable and plastic (Stuss and Knight 2013, p. 562). Executive function skills can be strengthened. We do have hope. With the right treatment and right approach, we can make incredible strides and speed up this troublesome delay.

Just like any sturdy set of pillars, standing strong against the dangerous elements, our Four Pillars need a stable foundation.

The Pillars' Foundation

There is a set of two very specific internal skills that are the foundation for all executive functions. Without these skills, and their ability to combine and work together, we do not have the Four Pillars or any chance for success. These skills are nonverbal working memory (NVWM) and verbal working memory (VWM).

Nonverbal working memory is a fancy medical term for the visual imagery system of the brain. It is the ability to create mental movies and hold them in mind. This is truly the skill that separates human beings from animals. By five years of age, human beings' nonverbal working memory system is stronger than all other living species (Levy 2024).

VWM works closely with NVWM. After engaging nonverbal working memory to visualize past experiences and future consequences, the brain shifts gears into verbal working memory. As the cognitive process responsible for managing self-talk, VWM guides us through tasks, regulates emotions, and allows us to make decisions with input from our inner voice—our ever-present "brain coach." VWM offers ongoing feedback, instructions, and encouragement.

These two skills, which we will refer to as the "foundation," help us to better understand some of the most problematic issues associated with ADHD, including time blindness, emotional dysregulation, and impulsiveness.

The pioneers of ADHD describe these foundational skills much better than I ever could—most notably, Dr. Russell Barkley and Sarah Ward, M.S., CCC-SLP. Without these two individuals, my understanding and knowledge of these skills would not be what it is today, and I most certainly would like to be able to help students as effectively as they have. Their work on these specific skills is groundbreaking and moving, and it completely changes the game when it comes to ADHD and executive function treatment.

With this new understanding of NVWM and VWM, we can better tailor treatments toward unique individuals and not take a "one-size-fits-all" approach simply because of a diagnostic label. By helping to strengthen these skills, we are giving our children and teens a mental Swiss army knife to help them fully utilize the Four Pillars and respond to life's inevitable obstacles as their best selves.

CHAPTER 2

The Foundation I

Nonverbal Working Memory and Visual Imagery

This is it—this is the skill. If there is one major thing I want you to take away from this playbook, it is an understanding of the importance of nonverbal working memory and its key role in ADHD and executive dysfunction.

The first aspect of nonverbal working memory is hindsight: our mental images of the past. As we go through life, specific experiences—people we meet, things we do—stick in our memories. These experiences not only stay with us, they help to guide our emotions, our feelings, and our personalities. We are what we remember. Our past is our story that shapes us. Without an image in our minds, these experiences cannot work to make us who we are.

Our NVWM gives us access to our memories. As Dr. Russell Barkley states, human beings have a movie theater in their minds, a mental DVD library of past experiences (ADHD Videos 2014b, 08:55). These are not just simple static "Google images" sitting still in your mind. They are true full-length feature film blockbusters. Within your mental movie, you see yourself moving through time and space, going through the experience. You see the world around you being altered, everything happening just as you lived it.

But it doesn't stop there. So much more flows from that image. As Dr. Barkley describes it, you can use your non-verbal working memory to remember that last time you went out to eat at a restaurant. You can create a full mental movie of that experience in your mind. From that image, with the power of NVWM, you are able to reinvigorate all of the senses. Not only can you see yourself at the restaurant enjoying your meal with your family and friends, you can also re-taste the foods, re-hear the sounds of the restaurant, re-feel the texture of the napkins, re-smell the aromas of each dish, and, most importantly, recall how this entire experience made you feel emotionally. All of these feelings flow from the image in our NVWM.

With the ability to revive all of the senses, we have something that is much more than just a collection of facts. We have a real experience that shaped us and can inform us for our future. By remembering our visit to that restaurant, we can gain a greater appreciation for the culinary arts and how to prepare certain foods. We can become a "foodie" and gain a new interest in various restaurants and types of foods. We can become incredibly curious about the restaurant industry and business. We can learn things we liked about this restaurant that will better prepare us to make decisions on where to eat in the future. We can start to invite peers out to eat with us and deepen our relationships beyond just calls, texts, and social media. We can learn to turn our phones off when we eat with others and enjoy their company while having a delightful meal.

This is the true beauty of life. All of this beauty flows from the images we can bring into our NVWM. This is why our past shapes us and defines who we are—because of these images and the deep feelings these images give us.

Think back on your educational journey from kindergarten to high school. What sticks in your mind? Do you remember a specific day in class when you learned something super cool and interesting? Or do you remember more of the unstructured social aspects of school? Great memories from the hallways, gym class, or recess? A funny joke that interrupted the lesson and caused the entire class to erupt in laughter? Your first crush and all the times you were so nervous talking to them?

There is a good chance you remember the unstructured moments. These are the ones that truly stick in your memory, because of the intense emotions tied to them. Because this is what human beings are all about: emotion. Our strong emotions are what drive us, move us, motivate us, and keep us going. This all starts with nonverbal working memory and the visual imagery system.

Of course, not all of these emotions will be positive. NVWM also encompasses our memories of trauma, bullying, and deep failures. It's quite fascinating how the negative memories stick in our minds the most. These are those incredibly hurtful or embarrassing memories that stay with us throughout our entire lives. The things that we know deep down, only we remember, only we keep with us, and only we think of as significant.

These are the memories that temporarily paralyze us when we are by ourselves, alone in the car, or in the shower. We freeze and make a weird noise to help us pass this negative memory as fast as possible. We might use a little negative self-talk to accept it and move on quickly. "Stupid, stupid, stupid!" We might even steal a page out of Jim Carrey's script from *Dumb and Dumber*: "You are one pathetic loser!" This helps to display what makes working memory so important—the intense emotions that are evoked when we reflect on previous experiences. These defining moments from our past stick with us and carry with them profound meaning.

The strength and importance of our ability to access hindsight in our nonverbal working memory cannot be overstated. This is the power to drive us to achieve real education in life, allowing us to grow, mature, and no longer act like a dependent child. When we remember what we previously did, whether positive or negative, it helps us to not only go through the same experiences again in a more effective way, it gives us resiliency and grit to handle different, but similar, experiences.

Episodic Memory

There is a special type of hindsight in nonverbal working memory that is difficult for ADHD brains. It carries significant importance toward developing productive life skills, executive functions, and a positive self-image. It is known as episodic memory. Episodic memories are your personal autobiographical memory of a specific event (Clayton et al. 2007). This is your personalized, one-of-a-kind definition of something.

For example, you can think of the basic Merriam-Webster definition of "birthday party"—a fun event where a loved one celebrates becoming one year older. We give them presents, and they open them while we cheer and take pictures. We also eat lots of tasty treats like cake and cupcakes.

An episodic memory might look more like this: "My cousin David had a birthday party. It was on the beach, and we had a huge bonfire! For dinner, we did a pig roast and ate barbecue. He had a live cover band that played oldies music and a huge dance floor."

If you were to think of a generic description of "summer camp," you might think something like "Summer camp is where you go when there is no school during the summer months. You go to a large field, play sports, and do outdoor activities. Sometimes you take bus trips to different locations."

You may also have an episodic memory of summer camp—an individualized recollection of something you personally experienced: "I went to summer camp in the Poconos. We weren't allowed to bring our phones or have access to any electronics. Every day, we were outside for hours. We would play various sports including kickball, pickleball, archery, and golf. At night, I slept in a log cabin with five other people. We would tell ghost stories all night to try to keep each other awake!"

Episodic memory is difficult for kids with ADHD due to a core deficit of visual imagery (ADHD Videos 2014b, 21:04). They're often lacking in overall self-awareness when the event was actually taking place, and they may not have the self-regulation to understand their emotions and see the cause-and-effect relationship between the event and how it made them feel.

Episodic memory is so incredibly important to the development of executive functions. The ability to understand things in our own unique individualized way allows us to tie our emotions to experiences and remember how certain events made us feel.

The following are some scenarios where an episodic memory can make all the difference.

ACADEMIC SETTING

Last month, you studied really hard for an upcoming test. You didn't cram last minute, you reviewed your work for several evenings before the test, and you received one of the highest scores in your life. Now, with another test coming up, you remember how successful that strategy was, and you decide to do the same thing this time.

SOCIAL EXPERIENCES

You had an amazing time going out sledding in the snow with your friends and neighbors. Each time you did it, you were able to pick up more speed instead of purposely slowing yourself down out of fear. Later in the week, your school announces it will have a ski trip. You remember how much fun you had in the snow and how amazing it felt to glide across it with incredible speeds. Instead of instantly disregarding the ski trip and saying, "Nah, I would rather go home and play Fortnite," you decide to sign up. You go on the ski trip and make several new friends. You and these new friends end up skiing together multiple times a year.

HOME ENVIRONMENT

Once, you got bored and needed some attention, so you went and provoked your sibling. This really annoyed them, so they lashed out at you and shoved you away. That instantly pushed you over the edge, so you physically attacked your sibling. Your parents then took away all your video games for a week. You didn't like how that felt. Next time you're bored and your sibling comes into sight, you have the idea to provoke them and get a rise out of them. But you decide not to do it because you are able to visualize how upset you were when your parents took those games away.

In these examples, we can see the second aspect of NVWM: foresight. Hindsight and foresight, or future thinking, are two sides of the same coin: hindsight is what allows us to learn from the past, and foresight is what allows us to imagine and plan for the future. We have to be able to envision ourselves in the future and have some sort of ability to use that vision to internally motivate ourselves.

Think about it—if I want to set a goal of losing 10 or 15 pounds, it will require a lot of self-motivation to learn to say "no" to all of the treats my wife buys for herself and leaves in the kitchen. The only way I am going to be able to achieve my goal is to stop, pause, and envision myself in the future looking skinnier and feeling much more healthy, positive, and accomplished. That mental image is what is going to drive me to delay gratification, get my mind off of what is most tempting now, and think about what is most beneficial for the long term—something my future self will thank me for.

If you are able to visualize the future, visualize the final result, know what you are working for because you can SEE it, you will have a much greater chance to self-regulate and self-motivate toward that end goal.

To fully understand how hindsight and foresight work together within NVWM, I highly recommend Dr. Russell Barkley's lecture at CADDAC, a group in Canada, that is available in full, for free, on YouTube. During this presentation, he breaks down ADHD and executive functioning in one of the most eloquent ways in all of human history. He spends almost 20 minutes alone discussing the importance of nonverbal working memory.

Let's look at a few more examples.

Being Late to School
- **Episodic memory:** I was late for school last week. I had to explain myself to the front desk and my teacher. When I walked into class, it felt like everyone was staring at me. That was not a good feeling.
- **Hindsight:** Being late made me feel embarrassed. I didn't like that experience, and I don't want to feel that way again.
- **Foresight:** I need to make sure I am not late anymore. I am going to set my alarm 20 minutes earlier and lay out my clothes the night before.

(continued)

Deleting YouTube

- **Episodic memory:** I decided to delete YouTube from my phone. The first few days afterward, my overall daily screen time went down by three whole hours. Since I wasn't on my phone so much, I was able to spend more time with my family and friends. I was also finally able to start reaching 10,000 steps a day!
- **Hindsight:** When I removed a major distraction, I had more free time, and I developed healthy habits. As a result, I was proud of myself, and I liked the way that felt.
- **Foresight:** I've made sure to stick to those habits every day since, and I'll never redownload the app.

Restoring Old Bikes

- **Episodic memory:** Instead of sitting and playing video games in the basement, my friends and I decided to restore our old bikes from our garages.
- **Hindsight:** We feel a strong sense of ownership and belonging to the bikes because we did the research and hard work to restore them ourselves. We now have a better understanding of how dedication and hard work can lead to pure joy.
- **Foresight:** Because of this memory, we are less likely to spend time playing video games, which typically just causes rage, yelling at the TV, and throwing the controller. Instead, we're more likely to devote our time and our lives to new and challenging activities that will bring us a sense of euphoria that cannot be gained from any video game.

The Core Foundational Skill

Nonverbal working memory *is* executive functioning. This is the core skill. All of those frustrating behaviors that you see in your child each day can be traced back to some aspect of NVWM.

You send your child upstairs to go clean their room. As soon as they enter their room, they get distracted by something they see, and nothing gets done. Why? An inability to visualize what their room will look like when it's clean so they can work toward that visual goal.

After every sports practice, your child is always happy and proud of himself that he went because he loves playing sports and has a lot of friends on his team. But every single day when it's time to go to practice, your child throws a major tantrum. Why? An inability to visualize being happy after practice and make choices oriented toward that outcome.

Your child gets home from school and instantly gets on screens instead of doing their homework. Why? An inability to visualize being done with homework, feeling proud, and then playing all the games they want once they are done, thus being unable to delay gratification until then.

You also see impulsive behavior constantly. You see this socially around peers, where they try to control everything in a way that instantly makes others not want to be around them. You see this at home where they rush to anger and use language that you would never repeat to your friends. To use a popular phrase, your child seems like they have absolutely "no filter." But that is just a catchy phrase. You know it is so much more serious than that.

What we have to understand is that all of these behaviors are related. All of them are tied back to NVWM. NVWM is the gateway to our past and our future. It is the true internal system of checks and balances. It is the true internal skill that allows us to utilize real information to keep us from making unhealthy choices. This *is* executive functioning.

Dr. Russell Barkley describes executive functions as a set of skills that allow you to "stop and think" and keep you from doing what you would have done on impulse (ADHD Videos 2014b, 00:33). This is every parent's goal: for their child to have an internal system of checks and balances that allows them to be healthy, independent, positive, and successful without adult assistance. This is the set of skills that is the greatest predictor of life success. Without NVWM, none of this is possible.

Our ability to create mental images and utilize mental movies is what motivates us, creates our emotions, drives our behaviors, and allows us to set and reach goals. Without mental movies, we cannot move through life with an upward trajectory, working toward a dream we have for our futures while also learning from our past mistakes. We would go through life as vagabonds, never knowing what is to come next or what we need to do to make ourselves happy, safe, and healthy.

This is one of the core skills that separates human beings from all other living species: the visual imagery system that allows us to visualize the past so deeply, learn from it, feel it, sense it. It's this system that allows us to make our tomorrows better than our yesterdays. This is what allows us to mature, grow, and gain the skills we need to be successful. This is how we learn more about ourselves, avoid repeating mistakes, and work toward our personal goals that are so near and dear to our hearts.

All executive functioning flows from an image from our visual imagery system. Executive functioning is the imagination.

CHAPTER 3

The Foundation II
Verbal Working Memory and Self-Talk

The foundation of the Four Pillars involves a second specific skill that must work in harmony with nonverbal working memory. These two skills are so crucial that without them, there will be no independence or meaningful success.

Together, these foundational skills are the true meaning of the incredibly vague phrase "stop and think."

First we become self-aware. Then we inhibit ourselves and stop responding based solely on external stimuli. We look within ourselves and visualize to ourselves. We use the hindsight in our NVWM to learn from our past experiences and to avoid repeating mistakes or behaviors that led to negative feelings such as isolation, sadness, shame, embarrassment, or competitive loss.

We then visualize ourselves in the future so that we can aim our behavior, emotions, actions, and choices toward that future. How can we do something now that helps us later? How can we make a choice now that will make our future self very happy and proud? All of this is part of NVWM.

Then—we talk to ourselves.

We engage in a dialogue, one that is silent, private, and fully internal.

We talk to ourselves and our brains, like we talk to others (exactly as we talk to others, in fact). But the dialogue is fully to ourselves, and only for us to hear.

This is verbal working memory (VWM): the ability to use self-directed speech to guide ourselves through various experiences, including the basic and mundane. Verbal working memory guides us through the many decisions, tasks, and emotions we face each and every day.

The Incredible Power of Self-Talk

What we have to understand is just how important this skill of verbal working memory and internalized speech truly is. Internalized speech is something that many people may not even realize is happening because it doesn't require conscious effort. But that little voice is always there, helping us navigate daily life.

Every waking moment, we are engaged in an internal dialogue, talking to ourselves and coaching ourselves through different situations. Before you even get out of bed in the morning, you're already having an internal conversation with yourself about how you need to get up, make the coffee, drink it, brush your teeth, get dressed, and get out the door by 8:15 a.m. so you can get to work before 9 a.m. And oh yeah, that project is due today, and I've barely done anything for it yet, so I should probably get there even earlier.

Our continuous internal dialogue is an essential function of VWM, guiding us step-by-step through our daily routines. This dialogue keeps us on track, helping us move smoothly from one task to the next.

But VWM isn't just about keeping your to-do list in mind. It functions as a mentor or guide inside your head, offering advice, reminders, and encouragement at every turn.

For example, when faced with a choice between watching TV or doing laundry so you have clean clothes for work the next day, your VWM might tell you: "If I do the laundry now, then I can relax and watch TV later." This kind of reasoning helps us delay gratification and make choices that align with our long-term goals.

Even when others are talking to us, we are constantly talking to ourselves. We are making sure we are listening and looking at them here and there, and we are preparing what we want to say before they even finish their sentence. We ensure the other person feels heard, appreciated, and understood. Our internal dialogue helps us with all of our relationships. It constantly tells our brains that the world does not revolve around us—other people matter, too.

This internal dialogue is never-ending. And it is always needed. As my friend Ryan The ADHD Dude frames it, it is our "brain coach" A Vince Lombardi, Bill Belichick, Tom Coughlin, Coach K, all inside our own mind.

VWM is particularly important during childhood and adolescence, as this is when we are developing the ability to regulate our own behavior and make more decisions independently. This internal skill is crucial for interacting with others, following social rules, and navigating the world effectively.

Here's the problem: kids and teens with ADHD tend to lag behind their peers in developing strong VWM. If you have a child with ADHD, you've seen the results of that delay, in the form of difficulties with impulse control, task completion, and social interactions.

A child with strong VWM might be able to say to themselves, "I'll need to get dressed, brush my teeth, and eat breakfast. I don't want to forget my backpack like I did last week. And I need to remember to pack my lunch, too."

But children with ADHD may have internal speech that is not as active or organized. Without a well-developed inner coach, these kids might get distracted after getting dressed, and there's a good chance they might end up forgetting to brush their teeth or pack their lunch. Their brain just isn't giving them the verbal prompts they need to stay on task. As a result, they might require more reminders and support from adults to complete their morning routine.

The absence of a "brain coach" is especially harmful for them because it can exacerbate natural tendencies toward impulsivity and distractibility. There are few phrases parents say to their ADHD child more than "just stop and think!" because of their intense impulsive behaviors that make adults cringe in embarrassment. By helping children to strengthen their internal dialogue, we give them a chance to do just that: "stop and think." Having a reliable "brain coach" allows these kids to function more independently and successfully in every environment they encounter.

Together, VWM and NVWM form the foundation of the executive functioning system. When both are developed and functioning well, children are better equipped to make thoughtful decisions, avoid impulsive behaviors, and achieve their goals.

The Barkley-Vygotsky Model

Lev Vygotsky is one of the most influential psychologists in history. He did his research and work during the early 1900s. All individuals who work with kids in any capacity should be familiar with his work. He is best known for his theory of cognitive development and the zone of proximal development.

The theory of cognitive development was an important milestone in our understanding of child development and how the brain learns. What made this theory groundbreaking, especially at the time, was that it helps to shed light on the importance of social interactions. Vygotsky stated that life's learning comes from social interaction and experiences with others, not so much from structured lectures and lessons from teachers (Cole et al. 1978). He stressed the importance of social negotiation and how we learn best about various topics by discussing them with others and learning their perspectives and their individual breakdown of the information.

This idea of "socialized learning" really challenged our concepts of how education works. At the time of Vygotsky's research, schools had truly barely changed over the course of a thousand years. Schools back then revolved around what I refer to as the "lecture-listen model." Teachers lecture for as long as possible about a given topic while students are asked to sit silently and listen. They are asked to store this information in their short-term memory and then regurgitate it on the next test or quiz. When the quiz is over, most of the information is out of their mind, and they are forced to move onto new information that will be on the next quiz.

Vygotsky's work challenged this notion entirely and flipped this idea about school on its head. His theory introduced the idea of "reciprocal learning" that is still popular today at Montessori schools. Reciprocal learning refers to a more social approach to learning in which the students and the teachers work together to understand concepts, instead of the teacher taking the lead role. According to Vygotsky, kids and teens learn best when they feel a sense of belonging, being part of a group, a team, or a society. This is more of a project-based learning approach, where students work together to understand and come together to discuss. Of course, with the way our public schools operate, we have chosen to mostly ignore this research. Sadly, many of the issues of Vygotsky's time still persist today.

Vygotsky then further contributed to the field of child development with his zone of proximal development, which explains basic skill development in children (Cole et al. 1978). There are specific things that a child can do independently, based on their age and overall skill level. Other things that they are not able to do on their own will require support from others until they have mastered them independently. This was the beginning of much of our understanding about executive functioning.

But it was Vygotsky's work on internalizing that really caught the attention of Dr. Russell Barkley. Vygotsky described internalizing as a transfer of information from one person to another, typically via external speech or external modeling. Over time, the information becomes internalized and becomes a facet of the child's knowledge and memory bank.

There is a particular part of this concept of internalizing where Dr. Barkley found a connection to executive functioning: the internalizing of speech.

> Vygotsky found a very specific timeline of this process (Rieber and Carton 1987):
>
> - **Ages 0–3:** Children emit language outwardly to others via expressive language that can always be heard and measured (no self-talk yet).
> - **Ages 3–5:** Children begin to talk to themselves out loud via an external language that can still be heard and measured (public).
> - **Ages 5–7:** The face and larynx become suppressed, and children start to develop internalized and privatized speech that can no longer be heard or measured. Language goes from *public to private*.
> - **Ages 9–12:** Children have full use of internal private language.

What Vygotsky does here is outline the process of speech going from external to internal. During the first five years of life, kids use language to interact with the world around them. They are learning the first few instances of the executive functioning skill of self-awareness. For the first time, they are learning that they have some control over their world. When I cry, Mom or Dad comes to me and gives me milk, holds me, or smiles at me and sings me a song. With language, noise emitted from the mouth, I can alter what happens around me.

During this time, kids will also use language to describe their world. This is the age when kids are constantly pointing out everything around them. I currently see this with my three-year-old daughter every day. Each time we go outside, she points out her favorite colors, flowers, trees, dogs, cats, and mail trucks. Kids are mostly using nouns at this time to describe what they see, and they are using language to share their energy and love for life, as they are experiencing things for the very first time.

It is during the ages of five to seven when the magic happens. This is the beginning of a foundational executive functioning skill that they will use every single day for the rest of their lives. During these ages, we start to see the face and the larynx become suppressed. In the beginning, children will talk to themselves with their mouths still moving as if they were talking out loud, but no sounds come out. A listener can no longer hear what they're saying. Since we can no longer hear it, we can no longer measure it either. This is the true definition of internalized and privatized.

Vygotsky laid the groundwork for this concept of learning known as internalization. Dr. Barkley studied Vygotsky's work and brought it into the purview of executive functioning. He took what Vygotsky learned about our youth and created his model for understanding ADHD and executive functions.

Just as speech becomes internalized, so does executive function. This is best shown in Dr. Barkley's image from his CADDAC lecture.

On the left side of the chart, we see the ADHD brain with executive dysfunction. On the right side, we see what a brain with strong executive functions is able to do. Dr. Barkley states that executive functions "will shift your behavior from the left to the right" (ADHD Videos 2014, 17:34). This is the process of executive function internalization—what can be referred to as the "Barkley-Vygotsky" model.

1. **External → Internal**
   - Executive dysfunction (or lack of skills due to young age): You are regulated by the external events around you.
   - Executive functioning: You are able to self-regulate via your thoughts (your visual imagery and internal speech).
2. **Others → Self**
   - Executive dysfunction: You are controlled by others.
   - Executive functioning: You are able to self-manage. As Dr. Barkley states, "You no longer need other people to wake you up in the morning."
3. **Temporal Now → Anticipated Future**
   - Executive dysfunction: You are preoccupied with the now, the present moment.
   - Executive functioning: You become more concerned about the future, and you are able to aim your behavior toward the distant future. The older you get, the further into the future you can visualize with your NVWM's foresight.

4. Immediate Gratification → Delayed Gratification
   - Executive dysfunction: You are concerned with only immediate consequences and what is most stimulating right now, in the moment.
   - Executive functioning: You have the ability to delay or defer gratification, and the ability to self-regulate and self-motivate toward the future.

In Dr. Barkley's words, "To summarize, this executive system is there to help you self-regulate and organize your behavior across time" (ADHD Videos 2014, 19:04).

This is what needs to be understood about people with ADHD and executive dysfunction—they are missing this internal system. This is what parents and teachers see every day in the form of external behaviors. This is why these kids are mislabeled as lazy, disinterested, and rude. This is why parents are so burnt out from dealing with the same behaviors every single day with the morning routine, homework, and evening routine. This is why the first thing you think of when you hear "ADHD" is "impulsive." They don't have the internal system to stop, think, and then do. They skip the "stop," don't have the "think" skills, and just *do*.

Two Skills in Harmony

Now you know why saying "why can't you just stop and think!" to your child with ADHD never works.

I've said it before, and I will say it again: "stop and think" is one of the most vague phrases of all time. It is truly:

1. STOP Self: Inhibit yourself from thought number one or Plan A, the first impulsive thought that comes to mind. You shut down the motor system and STOP.
2. VISUALIZE to Self: This is all with the power of non-verbal working memory. You create a mental movie in your brain. Reimage similar past experiences so you

can gain competence and confidence to help you get through a task or challenge in the present. You also make a mental movie of the future, visualizing what it might look like so you can better plan, prioritize, problem-solve, and delay gratification.
3. TALK to Self: Have an internal dialogue with your brain to help coach yourself through something new or difficult. Talk yourself through what you are visualizing so you can work toward that specific image.
4. DO: Initiate the task now that you have gone through and completed your internal system of checks and balances.

The absence of this system is ADHD. It's not an attention disorder, and definitely not an attention deficit. It is a disorder of executive functioning, and to be more specific, it is a weakness and disconnect in working memory. At first, this might sound a bit too scientific, causing many to not fully understand how serious this is. But this weakness and disconnect is very serious, and it is the foundational issue of ADHD.

When NVWM and VWM work together in harmony, we have executive functioning. When they're disconnected, we get larger problems that are much more noticeable to others than a lack of an internal skill.

One of the ways that this disconnect manifests is the absence of a concept known as conditional thinking. The best way to think of conditional thinking is IF → THEN. It is cause-and-effect thinking.

Conditional Thinking

Conditional thinking is all about weighing potential outcomes of decisions and understanding the consequences of actions before they occur. It involves the ability to visualize multiple possibilities, make predictions based on different variables, and adapt your behavior accordingly.

Conditional thinking is what allows a person to say:

"If I study now, then I can relax later."

"If I run this red light, then I might get a ticket."

"If I save money now, then I can afford something nice later."

Conditional thinking is a crucial component of decision-making, problem-solving, and delaying gratification. It's what allows someone to recognize the benefit of waiting for a reward. And it can't happen without NVWM and VWM.

Because of their deficit in NVWM and VWM, kids and teens with ADHD often live in the "now" rather than thinking ahead to the future. They make decisions without regard for the long-term effects. They act impulsively without considering alternatives.

This can have any number of negative results, including poor academic outcomes, strained social relationships, struggles with time management, and an inability to regulate their emotions based on an understanding of the future.

Children with ADHD often have a particularly hard time with delayed gratification, because they can't mentally hold onto the long-term reward and instead seek immediate satisfaction. Here's an example that might sound familiar to many of you: A child with ADHD just got a new video game that he's excited to play, and he also has homework due. Instead of thinking "If I finish my homework first, then I can play all afternoon," he goes straight for the Xbox, forgetting all about his homework.

When bedtime comes, he rushes through his assignment, making errors and skipping questions—if he does it at all. Tomorrow in class, he'll have to face the consequences of turning in incomplete work.

Let's look a little more deeply at how conditional thinking actually works. There is a thought process we go through every single day that sums up the executive function system perfectly. When you think about this specific phrase, you will better understand what executive functioning truly is and why ADHD is so debilitating.

> "If the future looks like that, then this is what I need to do now."

Think about that sentence for a few seconds—it is very powerful.

"If the future LOOKS like that, then this is what I need to do NOW."

If we break that down, we get:

- **IF:** Conditional statement
- **the future LOOKS like that:** Visual imagery with nonverbal working memory
- **THEN:** Identifying cause and effect
- **this is what I need to do:** Self-directed talk via verbal working memory
- **NOW:** Delaying gratification to get something done NOW to benefit you LATER

This is the thought process that kids and teens without ADHD are able to use unconsciously every day. It allows them to get things done without parent or adult assistance, accommodations, or intense dysregulation to finally get to the finish line. And the absence of this process is where the shame and negative self-image comes from kids with ADHD. They are not able to put the pieces of the puzzle together.

Why do I keep getting in trouble at school?

Why do I never get invited to birthday parties or sweet 16s?

Why do I never get invited to play at recess?

Why do I get picked on by others?

Why do I always fight with my parents?

Why can't I get off my phone or quit a video game?

Why do I always make the same stupid mistakes?

Why can't I just get this done?

Without the ability to have cause-and-effect thinking, we cannot connect our behaviors and words to their outcomes and consequences.

Our children and teens need to know how to visualize the past so they don't repeat mistakes. Visualize the future, so they can effectively plan, prioritize, problem-solve, and delay gratification. And as they persevere toward their goals, they must be engaged in positive, motivating self-talk to help guide their behavior toward a desired outcome.

It is the Four Pillars that many relate to when discussing ADHD behaviors. However, it is the foundational skills that allow the pillars to even exist. Nonverbal and verbal working memory are the essence of all executive functioning. Without the Foundation, the Four Pillars cannot stand.

PART I

Self-Awareness

CHAPTER 4

The First Pillar

Meet Sophie, an eight-year-old girl diagnosed with ADHD. Sophie is lively, curious, and always full of creative ideas, but there's one thing she consistently has a hard time with: self-awareness.

Her difficulty with self-awareness impacts her perception of her own behavior, her understanding of how her choices affect others, and her ability to monitor her actions in real time.

These struggles manifest in various parts of Sophie's day, affecting her academic performance, her home life, and her social relationships.

In the Classroom

Sophie is often told off by the teacher for talking to her classmates, not staying in her seat, or not paying attention. During lessons, she frequently blurts out answers without raising her hand. Her teacher constantly reminds her to wait her turn, but Sophie either doesn't notice that she's interrupting or doesn't understand why it's a problem.

It's not that Sophie is being intentionally rude. She's a good kid. She just genuinely isn't aware that her actions are disrupting the class, annoying her classmates, and impacting her own ability to focus.

She frequently gets frustrated because she doesn't understand why she's in trouble. From her perspective, she's just being herself—engaged, curious, and social.

Another example occurs during group activities. Sophie gets so caught up in her own excitement that she starts talking over her peers and taking control of the project. Despite the sighs, crossed arms, and frustrated looks from her classmates, Sophie doesn't change her behavior. She isn't able to pick up on these social cues, and she's confused when the others start avoiding her.

At Home

Sophie's lack of awareness extends to her daily routines. For example, when she's asked to clean her room, she may start the task but quickly get distracted by a toy or book. She genuinely believes she's been cleaning for a long time, when, in reality, she's spent most of the time playing. Her parents may come in to check on her progress, only to find that little has been done. Sophie is left feeling confused and overwhelmed when they tell her how much she has left to do.

With Friends

Sophie's social interactions are often strained because she doesn't notice when she's dominating conversations or ignoring others' ideas during games. Her friends might walk away or stop inviting her to play, but Sophie doesn't see why this happens. To her, everything seemed fine—she was just excited to share her ideas or take the lead in the game.

One afternoon during recess, Sophie and a group of friends are playing a game of tag. Sophie is so focused on winning that she starts bending the rules, tagging people before they're ready and running outside the designated play area. Several kids start to get upset, but Sophie doesn't see the problem. From her point of view, she's just trying to have fun. One of her classmates finally says, "You're not playing fair!"

Sophie feels hurt and confused. She didn't mean to break the rules—she just got caught up in the moment. The other kids stop playing with her, and Sophie spends the rest of recess alone, not fully understanding why the game ended or why her friends are mad at her.

She isn't able to monitor her own behavior, doesn't pick up on the cues indicating that her classmates are becoming frustrated, and struggles to understand how her actions led to a negative outcome.

Self-Awareness for the ADHD Brain

Self-awareness is the ability to understand and unconsciously feel our strengths, needs, likes, and dislikes. As we get older, our self-awareness stretches into social executive functions and perspective-taking skills. We start to become more aware of how we feel, how we make others feel, and how we are doing in social environments.

This skill first starts to develop at a young age. One of the most beautiful and amazing things about child development is when children become aware that they can have an effect on their environment. Young babies learn that when they cry, their parents will come to them, hold them, and possibly ease their hunger. As they get older, they learn that when they make noises, coo, and babble, their parents will make some noises in return. When they smile at their parents, they smile back. These are some of the most magical moments of early childhood.

Self-awareness is crucial to all executive function development, and as you can see, it is highly dependent on memory. Babies, toddlers, children, and teens need to be able to utilize their hindsight and remember past experiences to fully understand how their environment works and their own individual effect on it. Because kids with ADHD struggle with the foundational skill of hindsight, their self-awareness often lags well behind their peers.

The lack of self-awareness can be so incredibly hard on kids and teens with ADHD. We see this sprout up in a number of ways. The high schooler who comes home from school every day to play Fortnite with peers, thinking they are his real friends, although they never invite him to hang in person when they get together: The preschooler or elementary student who bosses peers around during unstructured playtime and is incredibly rigid in their play schemes. The middle schooler who will go to great lengths just to make someone laugh, because if they can make someone laugh, that person will surely like them. That laugh they hear gives them a dopamine rush that is just so fulfilling. However, without self-awareness, it is far too difficult to know if they are laughing with you, or laughing at you. There is a good chance it's the latter.

If we want to improve any skill in life, we first have to be self-aware. If we want to get a new job, make more money, pay the bills, or take a needed break—we first have to be self-aware.

It's no exaggeration to say that self-awareness is part of nearly everything we do. One specific area where self-awareness has a huge impact is on the ADHD brain's relationship to time.

The Time Horizon and Time Blindness

As a parent to a child with ADHD, there's one thing you probably notice every day: a total inability to sense time, feel time, understand it. Morning routines, bedtime routines, homework after school—all a complete mess.

Without you, they would be late to everything. Nothing would get done. They would be failing every single class. They would never shower or brush their teeth. No sense of time, no sense of urgency.

This comes down to two factors: a shortened time horizon and time blindness.

Simply put, a time horizon is the mental window through which a person can project into the future. It's how we envision events and make plans based on how far away those events are. It's the ability to think ahead, anticipate consequences, and prepare for future needs.

A long time horizon is what allows us to schedule tasks and activities based on both immediate and distant goals. For example, if you have a project due in two weeks, having a clear sense of that timeline and spacing out your work accordingly helps ensure that you're ready when the due date comes. You can break the project down into smaller steps, create a plan, and stick to it. When the deadline arrives, you have a high-quality project that shows off your hard work. Take away your long time horizon, and all of that falls apart.

People with a well-developed time horizon can juggle multiple responsibilities and prioritize them according to urgency. They understand when to start tasks and how to fit them into their schedules without being overwhelmed.

A time horizon is all about allowing us to understand the future before it arrives. That also means helping us to understand the consequences of our choices before we make them. This doesn't just apply to school or work—it includes consequences in our social and personal lives, too. If we want someone to come to our birthday party next week, then we probably shouldn't impulsively comment on how much we hate their new haircut. But a constricted time horizon makes it hard to see how the choices we make right now influence what happens next.

It's normal for our time horizon to change as we grow up. Young children will have a very short time horizon, and it will expand as they become more mature. A well-developed time horizon starts to be important as kids get older and take on more commitments. A teen might need to balance extracurricular activities, homework, and chores. If they have a two-week time horizon, they can allocate time for each responsibility, ensuring none of their commitments are left to the last minute. If they have a time horizon of just one day, it's going to be almost impossible for them to think ahead and arrange their schedule in a way that leaves enough time for everything to get done.

Children and teens with ADHD have a greatly reduced time horizon compared to their same-age peers. They can only think about and plan for the current moment or very near future, so they are limited in their ability to set goals and anticipate outcomes. As a result, they might struggle in school, experience social difficulties, deal with emotional instability, or fail to meet their long-term goals.

As executive function specialists Sarah Ward and Kristen Jacobsen state so well: Many people with ADHD struggle with a basic awareness of time because they have only two modes: "now" and "not now." This lack of an intuitive sense of time means people with ADHD risk being stuck in the "now" and forgetting about the future—until it's too late.

Future events or deadlines feel distant and intangible until they suddenly become immediate and unavoidable (ADHD Videos 2014, 20:45). Even though they may know they have a bill that's coming up due or a major project with an approaching deadline, they won't feel any urgency to address that future event until it's right in front of them. Quite often, the result is an avoidable crisis.

When you live life stuck in "now" mode, the long-term consequences can be significant. Chronic lateness, procrastination, and missed deadlines can lead to academic challenges, and, later on in life, job loss or missed career opportunities. Financially, forgetting to pay bills or file taxes on time can result in penalties. Socially, showing up late to events, or missing them entirely, may strain relationships of all kinds. Managing responsibilities, planning for the future, making informed decisions—none of it is possible without this ability to peer into the future.

Another major factor affecting kids and teens with ADHD is time blindness. Time blindness refers to difficulty perceiving, managing, and estimating time. The term was coined by Dr. Barkley, and it is a hallmark symptom of ADHD (Barkley 2015).

While neurotypical people may have an intuitive sense of how much time is passing or how long a task will take, people with ADHD frequently struggle to do the same. Time remains abstract, either slipping away too quickly or stretching out into a never-ending expanse. Time blindness is the root of problems related to hyperfocus, task paralysis, and difficulty following daily routines. We'll go into each of these in more detail in the next chapter.

Many people with ADHD feel incredibly stressed, frustrated, and guilty because of their struggles with time. They might face judgment or criticism from others, which only worsens their self-esteem.

This is just as true for parents with ADHD as it is for kids. Parents might feel constant shame and guilt for being late to pick their child up from school or missing school events. No matter how much they care about their child, no matter how much they want to be there on time, their time blindness gets in the way. This can lead to a cycle of self-criticism fueled by feelings of anxiety and inadequacy.

It's not that people with ADHD don't care. It's that ADHD directly prevents them from perceiving and managing time the way other people do.

Screens and Executive Functioning

Wake up, go to school, come home, stay home. This has become the new daily life for the American child. The children have come inside, and they've stayed there. In their room, in the basement. Playgrounds, forests, basketball courts, soccer fields, and backyards have become desolate. Swing sets are empty, swaying only from the wind. Bike stores are filled with unused inventory, just waiting for a child to come and start riding.

The children are where they are *not* supposed to be. Indoors.

> "Play is the work of childhood."
> —Mr. Rogers

Children now spend far less time outside than previous generations (Clements 2004), most often with some type of screen right in front of their face. They are no longer going outside, looking far down the street, down through the woods, or across the field at a park. An interesting fact is that today's youth is facing a significant rise in near-sightedness. This is especially true for school-age children, and it's a direct result of decreased time outdoors and increased screen time (Alvarez-Peregrina et al. 2020). This is just one significant negative example of how screens are so incredibly unhealthy for their young developing minds and bodies.

Children being home all day is not healthy for their ability to gain life skills. We cannot talk about the development of executive functions without addressing the modern epidemic of screen use.

One thing we know about the ADHD brain is that it handles dopamine differently than the neurotypical brain

(Volkow et al. 2011). Dopamine is a chemical messenger that is released by the brain when you do something enjoyable. It acts on areas of the brain to give you feelings of pleasure, satisfaction, and motivation. Dopamine also has a role to play in controlling memory, mood, sleep, learning, concentration, movement, and other body functions (Cleveland Clinic 2022).

Here is the conundrum: to kids with ADHD, screens are just so unbelievably stimulating. They offer the ability to get an extra dose of dopamine with the swipe of a finger on a touchscreen or by pushing a button on a controller.

The stimulation is far too powerful for a young brain, especially for a young neurodiverse brain that already struggles with delays in executive functions and time blindness. Just as loud crowded rooms can be far too stimulating for neurodiverse kids, all of those screens in your home may be doing the same thing to your ADHD child.

It's as simple as this. When it comes to screens, their brains aren't ready for what we are giving them.

Screens to ADHD are just like a slot machine to the gambling addict, or a bottle of vodka to the alcoholic. Every single thing about screens seems like it was designed specifically for the ADHD brain. When you introduce screens into the life of an ADHD child, you are setting yourself up for a hell of a lot of dysregulation, fighting, isolation, negotiating, and noncompliance. Nothing will ever be able to stimulate their brain the way that the screen does.

When I say "screens," I'm not necessarily talking about every screen in your house. Not all screens are equally damaging. Let's break down exactly what a "screen" is, which ones are okay, and which ones are too dangerous.

The following are addictive and dangerous screens:

- Video games (Xbox, PlayStation, Switch)—most especially online video games where you play with or against others over the Internet
- Computer games
- YouTube (especially videos of other people playing video games)
- Social media (especially apps that involve quick videos like Instagram and TikTok)
- Smartphones
- Tablets
- Virtual reality games
- Screen-based Amazon Alexas

Less dangerous and addictive screens include:

- Television (if you can delete the YouTube app from your smart TV, even better. Yes, it is possible to do. Don't give up, you will figure it out!)
- Audiobooks
- Kindles
- Amazon Alexa/Google Home (with no screen)
- Video games from before 2005 (Nintendo 64, Super Nintendo, GameCube, PlayStation 1—old video games that are not online or connected to the internet)
- Family movie night (highly recommended for family bonding activity)
- Active movement games like "Wii Sports" or "Just Dance"
- Smart watches
- Apple AirTags to track your kids so they don't need a phone

Yes, most often, you can keep the TV in your house. Think back to the nineties when television was the only true screen in our homes. We watched it a lot, but it did not cause the intense problems we are seeing with today's youth. Watching a lot of TV also did not keep you from going outside. TV is a less stimulating screen that you will eventually get bored with, and you'll feel a desire to get up and move. The commercials come up, the show gets boring, so you get up and use your imagination and creativity to do something else. Video games and touchscreens are not giving these breaks of boredom like TV did.

The dangerous and addictive screens outlined here have a profound negative influence on each of the Four Pillars, including self-awareness.

Because of how the ADHD brain processes dopamine, kids and teens with ADHD are at heightened risk of problematic screen use and addiction-like behavior (Werling et al. 2022). Digital addiction changes the function and structure of developing brains. The most affected part of the brain is the prefrontal cortex (Ding et al. 2023)—the area that governs executive functions. Digital media's combination of instant gratification and low-demand tasks severely limits kids' abilities to gain vital lifelong self-awareness skills like self-monitoring and situational awareness.

Media multitasking degrades the foundational skill of working memory (Baumgartner et al. 2014). Constant interruptions from notifications, switching apps, and multitasking deplete working memory, reducing kids' ability to self-monitor, reflect on the past, and make plans for the future.

If a child is able to easily escape into the virtual world of screens, they will not have the downtime to sit, be bored, and think about their lives. Remember, executive functioning is a fancy term for the imagination. When do we use our imagination? When we are bored.

When kids are bored, they use their past memories and think about what could have gone differently. Without the stimulation of screens, they are left with only their thoughts and forced to learn how to self-monitor and be self-aware. This is the perfect opportunity to develop visual imagery (NVWM) and self-talk (VWM). This will give them more time to think about their performance in school, sports, or other areas of their life and what can be changed.

This is true organic and natural practice for strengthening the executive function system. Being bored is one of the most healthy and positive things for kids and teens. It's a time when they develop skills. If they have screens, they never have to experience boredom. If they have screens, they will likely not develop crucial executive function skills at the necessary pace. Now that we've covered the fundamentals of self-awareness, we can look at some tactics for strengthening this key executive function. In the next chapter, you'll learn how to reduce screen time, implement self-monitoring strategies, and develop a framework for consequences that actually helps kids understand their own behavior.

CHAPTER 5

The Playbook on Self-Awareness

A lack of self-awareness can be incredibly damaging for kids and teens with ADHD. Luckily, these kids and teens aren't helpless, and neither are you.

Without self-awareness, children will particularly struggle with self-monitoring, situational awareness, and understanding consequences. For each of these problems, there are several ways we can support them at home and in the classroom to help them strengthen executive functioning and improve their quality of life.

Self-Monitoring

One major component of self-monitoring is time blindness. Kids and teens who struggle with time blindness may find that their to-do list feels insurmountable. This is known as task paralysis, where the sheer number of tasks they need to accomplish becomes so overwhelming that nothing gets done at all.

Because they have difficulty estimating how long things will take, it's a challenge to understand how to fit everything into their day. They might have trouble breaking these tasks down into smaller, more manageable steps and figuring out which task should take priority. Instead of tackling their to-do list, they end up—well, paralyzed. They feel frozen, scrolling through their phone for hours instead of getting started.

If task paralysis is an inability to do any tasks at all, hyperfocus is being able to do *just one task* to the detriment of everything else. Hyperfocus involves someone becoming so engrossed in an activity that they lose track of time completely. The idea of people with ADHD focusing too much might seem like a strange paradox, but it's actually a direct result of time blindness.

This extreme focus on one activity can cause them to neglect other responsibilities. In this state, hours can pass without them realizing it. They might miss appointments, forget meals, or lose sleep. The world around them disappears as they remain completely absorbed in their own world.

Hyperfocus, time blindness, and task paralysis all tie back to the ADHD brain's shortened time horizon. An underdeveloped time horizon makes it almost impossible to stay motivated toward anything that involves being rewarded later instead of right now. This is so harmful, especially for older kids and teens who might want to start pursuing bigger or more ambitious goals.

For example, making the varsity basketball team might require a disciplined training regimen that is followed day after day. That kind of consistency can be out of reach for kids with ADHD, because the reward for all of that work feels far off and abstract compared to the "now" they're living in. Deadlines for college applications, scholarships, internships: it all requires self-monitoring and a strong awareness of time.

It's so hard to see this as a parent or a teacher. You might know that a teen is a talented artist and loves art class—but even so, they repeatedly fail to turn in assignments on time or at all. No matter how encouraging you are, they just don't have the self-monitoring and long-term thinking to commit to succeeding at something they love.

As frustrating as this is for adults to see, it can be even more frustrating for the kids themselves. Constantly missing deadlines, being late, or feeling overwhelmed by last-minute tasks can take a serious toll on their self-esteem. They may feel like they're always going from one crisis to the next. Eventually, they might start believing they just can't keep up with their peers and perceive themselves as less capable than others, even if that's not true.

But when we help kids develop their self-monitoring abilities, we empower them to be their best selves.

A big part of developing the ability to self-monitor is simply practice. While some kids and teens will naturally develop a "brain coach" that's checking in on them and making sure they remain on task, kids and teens with ADHD often won't gain this self-monitoring skill without some extra help.

That can be as easy as giving them examples of what a good "brain coach" sounds like. Once they hear those prompts externally enough times, they can start to internalize them. We can break these "brain coach" prompts into three categories: before the task, during the task, and after the task.

Keep the prompts short and sweet. You can display them on printed laminated cards and have kids respond to them verbally, or you can have them write down their answers so they have a record of their responses to review later. When you're using this strategy, the task in question should be short—no more than about 15 minutes. As kids build up their self-monitoring skills, they can work for longer stretches at a time. But start small.

> Pre-task prompts might sound like this:
>
> What's my goal for this task?
> What might get in my way?
> How am I feeling about this task?

This last prompt can actually help identify underlying causes of procrastination or other negative behaviors. If a child says they "just don't want to do" something, it may turn out that what they're really feeling is overwhelmed. Remember task paralysis?

By checking in about how they feel, you might learn that they're avoiding getting started because they just don't know how to begin. Step in and help them chunk work to reduce that feeling of being overwhelmed and get them past their paralysis.

During the 15-minute working period, encourage students to quickly pause and rate how focused they feel on a scale of 1 to 5. They can also ask themselves questions like the following.

> Am I doing what I said I would do?
>
> Is it easy for me to focus?
>
> How do I feel?

When you first start doing these exercises, it's likely that at some point during the 15 minutes, you will see that the child is getting off-task. One thing that's not going to help here? A verbal reprimand. That's just going to distract them further and keep them from getting back on track.

A better way to guide them back to the task is to establish a private signal system. Work with the child to come up with a nonverbal cue that you can give if you see their attention start to stray. The cue can be something simple, like a subtle hand sign or a tap on the desk. This is a great way to remind the child to refocus without causing further dysregulation or embarrassment in front of their peers. The faster you can make them aware that they've gone off-task, the better they'll become at recognizing it in themselves. Just make sure you work out this signal system *before* they start the task, so that it's in place and ready to go when you need it.

> After the 15 minutes is over, follow up with equally brief post-task prompts. Here are some examples:
>
> Did I accomplish my goal?
> What worked well for me?
> What would I do differently next time?

In addition to using these prompts at the end of a 15-minute working period, you can do something similar at the end of the school day, or at the end of a larger nonpreferred task at home. A short, one-minute daily self-reflection can be an excellent building block for self-monitoring. These reflections provide opportunities for kids to pause and think back on their behavior overall.

> Prompts for a quick daily self-reflection routine might include:
>
> What kind of student was I today?
> What did I notice about how I reacted when I was frustrated?
> How well did I succeed in meeting my goals?

When used consistently, these strategies can help kids develop self-monitoring skills and demonstrate on-task behavior with fading prompts toward independence.

I want to draw your attention to this last phrase—it's important. According to the GrowNOW model of internal skills, all goals are written with the phrase "with fading prompts toward independence." This is to ensure that the focus always remains the same: on internal skill building, not endless accommodating. To do this, we will need to use the following prompt hierarchy:

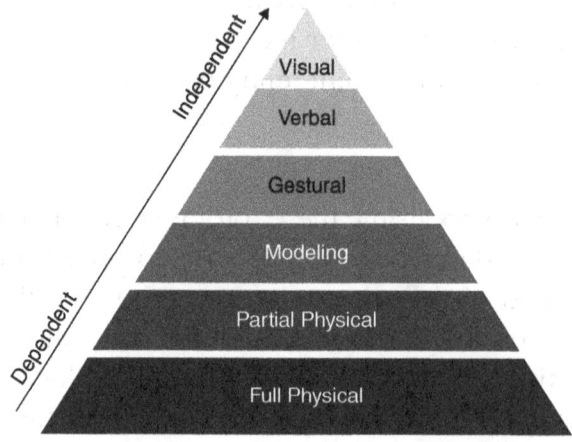

This image represents all prompting, from maximum to moderate to mild, and finally to full independence. The goal is to always be aware of the intensity of the prompts needed to ensure the child is successful at a particular task, as well as the number of times that prompt is needed.

This system also makes data collection a lot easier for the educator. They are able to simply label the prompt that was given and the number of times it was needed for the child to be successful. As success is gained, the educator will be able to move their way up the pyramid toward full independence for the task. Once this is reached, accommodations or interventions are no longer needed, and the child has acquired a new skill that they will be able to utilize throughout their life.

You'll notice that in this hierarchy, verbal prompting comes before visual prompting. After you've provided verbal self-monitoring prompts for some time, you can try progressing to the use of a visual monitoring tool during timed tasks. Visual monitoring tools can include a visual timer or progress tracker, like a to-do list with an estimated time required for each step. This is a great method to help kids move up that pyramid toward independence.

Situational Awareness in Social Settings

Self-awareness is essential for a healthy social life. Without being aware of ourselves and how we make others feel, it's extremely difficult to form meaningful relationships. If you're not present, engaged, and situationally aware, you'll struggle to pick up on body language, facial expressions, or other subtle cues that indicate annoyance, boredom, or frustration. And if you can't do that, you won't realize when your behavior is bothering those around you.

Like self-monitoring, true situational awareness requires a well-developed time horizon.

If we have an inability to think ahead and manage time, we're more likely to be late, forget commitments, or let plans fall through. This can make kids and teens with ADHD, with their limited time horizon, seem unreliable and untrustworthy, even though their behavior isn't intentional.

Here's a real-life example: A teen with ADHD promises to hang out with a friend, but by the time the scheduled meetup arrives, they've forgotten all about their plans. After they do this more than once, their friend feels hurt and starts to pull away, believing that they must not really care about the friendship.

Another major part of situational awareness is conditional thinking. This is what allows someone to step back and consider the consequences of their choices before acting. Without it, successful socializing is a nearly impossible task.

Parents of kids with ADHD often get a firsthand view of this, and it can be heartbreaking for them to see. Their kids will show impulsive behaviors and poor judgment in social situations, frequently interrupting conversations and acting with no regard for their peers' feelings. Without conditional thinking, they can't anticipate how their actions will impact others. And, due to that same lack of situational awareness, they have trouble seeing when their peers feel ignored, annoyed, or upset. Over time, these patterns of behavior will harm friendships as other children begin to view them as inconsiderate, disruptive, or just plain mean—even when you, as their parent, know that's not true.

We really see this come out during conflicts. A child with strong conditional thinking skills will understand the effects of their behavior toward other people: "If I yell at my sibling, then they'll get even more mad, and our argument will just get worse." But for children without this foresight, emotional reactions can rapidly spiral into bigger conflicts.

To develop situational awareness and improve social skills, children need to spend time in social settings with other kids. There's no way around it. It is the only way to strengthen this ability.

For many kids, that means eliminating, or at least severely limiting, screen time.

Listen: I get it. I know you had good intentions. You gave your child a smartphone so they could be like their peers, thinking it would help them socially. But now, that phone is far more stimulating than a peer could ever be.

A kid's perspective goes something like this: "When I am with a peer, I have to stop, be quiet, look at them, listen to them, be flexible, be kind, and do things they want to do. When I have this smartphone, I am in complete control. I don't have to share anything with anyone. I don't have to do anything I don't want to do. I choose the games and videos, all with the swipe of a finger. Now that I have this phone, everything else is boring and stupid. Going outside, joining after-school activities, having conversations with my parents—thanks, but no thanks."

Screens are experience killers, and experiences are how executive functions are developed.

You are the parent. You brought those screens into the house. You pay the bills for the phone, the electricity, and the Wi-Fi. Without you, none of those screens would be there. You brought them in, it's your responsibility to take them out.

You might be thinking "But screens are how they socialize. If I remove screens, they'll lose all their friends and become isolated or socially rejected." Here's the reality: If you encourage your child to develop in-person friendships instead of online ones, they'll be far more likely to gain social skills and form healthy, long-lasting bonds. Because the truth is, social media isn't social. Staring at a screen is no replacement for interacting with another human being. Studies tell us that overexposure to digital screens actively harms, not helps, the development of social skills (George et al. 2023).

When you limit screens and insist that your child spends more time with peers—whether through sports, a club at the rec center, or an after-school activity you sign them up for—they're not going to like it. And that's hard to deal with. It can be difficult for parents to see their children unhappy. But don't confuse temporary unhappiness with actual harm. Your child will be upset about losing screens, but they won't be harmed—in fact, just the opposite. Screens themselves are what's causing the harm.

Remember that your child's immediate satisfaction is not a measure of your abilities as a parent. It's much more important to give them the opportunity to develop the social skills and situational awareness they need to be successful in life.

Understanding Consequences

This is a common, debilitating symptom of ADHD for kids and teens. Too often, there's a complete inability to connect the behavior they're displaying right now to negative outcomes in the future.

It doesn't matter how many times you explain to them what will happen if they fight with their siblings, blow off their chores to play video games, or miss the school bus in the morning. It doesn't matter if they experience bad grades, punishments, or embarrassment in front of their peers. They just can't seem to understand the consequences of their actions.

We see this all the time in academic contexts. Without the self-awareness to picture themselves in the future, students with ADHD often procrastinate and struggle to keep up with assignments, projects, and exams. They don't feel any urgency to start tasks that are not immediately required, which, as we've all seen, can result in stress, anxiety, and frustration at the eleventh hour.

Time blindness means that children with ADHD often have trouble estimating how long tasks will take. Combine that with a shortened time horizon, and they have even more difficulty planning ahead. Because they're likely to underestimate how much time is needed, when they finally start something, it may already be too late to finish on time.

For example, a teen with ADHD might think that writing their history essay will take only an hour. But when they begin writing, they realize it will take much longer. Because they didn't plan ahead, they end up either missing sleep or submitting late work.

The same thing often happens with daily routines. Kids and teens with ADHD may struggle to maintain a set schedule due to an inability to gauge how long they need to complete all the steps in their routine. They might consistently underestimate how long it will take to get dressed, eat breakfast, and prepare for the day.

Conditional thinking is a big part of this, too. It's difficult to set up your day for success when you don't see the cause-and-effect relationship between preparation and positive results. Without this ability, mornings are chaotic and rushed—every day.

These kids don't have the cognitive processes to work backward from what will happen if they get behind schedule: they'll get yelled at by their parents, miss their bus, and have to sign in late at the office. Those potential consequences just don't "sink in" in a way that motivates them to stick to their morning routine.

Another aspect of this is an inability to prioritize when there are multiple tasks to complete. Kids without ADHD might develop a natural sense of how to prioritize activities based on deadlines or importance. But for kids who have ADHD, everything feels equally urgent, or conversely, nothing feels urgent at all until the last possible moment.

They're just not self-aware enough to monitor their actions, look into the future, plan ahead, and take the steps needed to avoid negative outcomes.

Dr. Russell Barkley openly discusses that individuals with ADHD will actually need more consequences to help them stay on task, learn, and develop skills (ADHD Videos 2014, 13:20). Unfortunately, this is just the opposite of what is happening in the schools today. We are seeing a widespread change toward decreasing and eliminating consequences. From my experience, this is happening for a number of reasons.

First, parents' complaints and lawsuits are sharply increasing. Too many schools now often find themselves in defense mode, to the point that they will do whatever they can to appease the parents and limit complaints and lawsuits. This is pressure sent directly to the school leadership: directors of special services, principals, and superintendents. The school leadership team then informs the teachers what they need to do to ensure these complaints stop. This puts teachers, who of course are overworked and underpaid (Google teacher salaries in your area), in lose-lose situations. They are often trying to assist this child with special needs while also juggling all the other students in their classroom, many of whom also have their own IEPs or 504s.

Second, due to the hectic and busy schedule so many teachers and educational professionals find themselves in, they often do not have the time, resources, or support to deal with behaviors and other issues in the most appropriate or evidence-based manner. Due to this, many teachers' "go-to" consequence for an issue that happens at school is to simply inform the parents. For example, a teacher may call or email a parent if a child says something inappropriate to them or a classmate, gets an F on a test, cuts class, or gets significantly behind on schoolwork. The teacher will fill the parent in on what is happening, in hopes that the parent will work on this directly with the child and hold them accountable at home. But if the child has ADHD, this most often will not work.

We have to remember: ADHD is a disorder of working memory. These individuals are stuck in the now, stuck in the present moment. We are asking the parents, in the home, to hold the child accountable for something that took place in a different location, around different people, at a different time—often hours before.

Good luck. Not going to help.

Consequences for ADHD kids and teens need to be immediate. If there is a delay, it further hurts their ability to connect the behavior with the consequence.

Does this mean parents shouldn't hold them accountable? Absolutely not. If for some reason they do have access to a smartphone, video games, or other screens, that should be removed indefinitely until this behavior is resolved. They should be given extra chores to do, or things along those lines. But this cannot be the be-all and end-all.

We need the consequences to come at school, from the individuals who have a much more structured relationship with the child as compared to the parent. When it comes to the ADHD brain, school is school, and home is home.

As Dr. Barkley says, kids with ADHD need increased accountability and more consequences, not fewer. This is how the internal skills are developed so that both the negative behavior is eradicated and adult support can fade out over time. For these children, consequences should balance clearly defined, structured expectations with opportunities for skill-building. The goal is to help kids and teens develop self-awareness and executive functioning skills in a supportive way that fosters true independence.

The following is a framework for consequences that can be implemented by teachers and education professionals.

It is designed to increase accountability while discouraging inappropriate behaviors and, most importantly, promoting personal growth.

- **Logical consequences:** Consequences work best when they're directly connected to the behavior that needs to be changed (Matthews 2017). For example, if a student is off-task during class and doesn't finish their schoolwork, they should use a structured study hall period to finish it. If their work is still not done at the end of the day, require the student to stay after school to finish it.
- **Reflection and action plans:** Implement a "three-step reflection." First, have the student identify what went wrong (e.g., talking to friends during class prevented them from finishing their work on time). Then, brainstorm one action to fix the problem (help the student recognize that they will need to use class time more wisely). Finally, ask the student to commit to one strategy to prevent it from happening again (provide the student with some of the self-monitoring strategies described earlier in this chapter to stay focused during independent work sessions).
- **Progressive steps toward accountability:** For minor infractions, provide a verbal warning and re-teach expectations. After repeated infractions, notify the student's parents and set up a meeting to discuss accountability strategies. For ongoing issues, a behavior contract that details specific expectations and consequences can be effective.

PART II

Self-Regulation

CHAPTER 6

The Second Pillar

What You Deal with Most Often

Meet Liam, a 10-year-old boy who is bright, energetic, and full of potential. But because of his ADHD, he often struggles with self-regulation, particularly when it comes to managing his emotions. He has an especially hard time controlling his anger, and this is a major problem at home with his parents. His emotional outbursts often come on quickly and intensely, leaving both him and his parents feeling frustrated and overwhelmed.

Morning Routine Battles

Every morning is a challenge for Liam. His parents try to keep a consistent routine: wake up, get dressed, have breakfast, and head to school. However, Liam often feels overwhelmed by the transition from sleeping to getting ready. If his mother tells him to hurry up and get dressed, it can trigger a big reaction: "Why do I have to get ready now? I'm still tired!" Instead of getting dressed, Liam might throw his clothes on the floor and refuse to cooperate. What could be a simple task turns into a 20-minute argument filled with tears and shouting.

Homework Meltdowns

Liam's parents have a "homework first, then screen time" rule. But after a long day at school, Liam feels exhausted and heads straight to his video games. When his parents remind him about his homework, he shouts, "I hate homework! I'm not doing it!" And if his parents enforce their rule, Liam's frustration escalates to the point that he kicks his backpack, slams his fists on the table, and screams, "You're the worst parents ever!"

Arguments Over Limits

One weekend afternoon, Liam is playing his favorite video game. He's completely engrossed in it and feels proud of himself for getting past a difficult section. He's just started a new level when his mom asks him to turn off the game because they need to leave for a family outing.

Immediately, Liam feels a surge of frustration. He's not ready to stop, and his internal dialogue isn't well-developed enough to help him calm down and regulate his emotions. Instead, his anger takes over. He yells, "No! It's not fair! I'm not stopping!"

When his mom insists, Liam's frustration escalates into a full-blown tantrum. He throws the controller onto the floor and storms off, slamming his bedroom door.

Liam feels a mix of overwhelming frustration and helplessness. He can't understand why stopping the game feels so devastating in the moment, and the emotions are too big for him to manage. It takes Liam a long time to calm down. By then, the family outing has been delayed, leading to more stress for everyone.

Self-Regulation Deficit Disorder

Self-regulation is quite possibly the most important of the Four Pillars. This is truly ADHD in a nutshell. Enough with this "hyperactivity" nonsense. Looking at ADHD as an external behavior-based disorder has gotten us nowhere.

Right now in the DSM, there are three subtypes of ADHD:

- Hyperactive type
- Inattentive type
- Combined type

But let me simplify all this for you, using this new focus on self-regulation:

- Hyperactive: Difficulty self-regulating your body
- Inattentive: Difficulty self-regulating your thoughts
- Combined: Difficulty self-regulating both

It's all self-regulation. Dr. Russell Barkley often refers to ADHD as *self-regulation deficit disorder* (Barkley 2022). It is important to note that this is also the most common symptom and what parents report back to me the most. I hear about their child's anger, outbursts, tantrums, terrible language, physical aggression, destruction of property, and attacks on their siblings.

The most common aspect of ADHD is also sadly the least understood. Countless families have told me they have spent thousands on evaluations just to get recommendations for preferential classroom seating and extended time on tests for a 504 or IEP. Prestigious doctors and neuropsychologists continue to view ADHD as a disorder that will only affect kids at school and impact their ability to listen to lectures, get work done, get good grades, and study. Parents often report that their doctor tells them to only give kids their meds on school days—don't worry about weekends or over the summer: "We only need her to pay attention in school."

This is why parents end up seeing massive behaviors in the home, behaviors that are so extreme they don't even know how to start dealing with them. They think to themselves, "I was told he only had ADHD, and this would only affect him at school—why is this happening at home?"

This then often leads parents to Facebook groups because it's a lot easier to get answers and validation there, compared to an expensive doctor with a six-month waiting list who, when you finally get into their office, wants you in and out as quickly as possible. When parents turn to social media groups, they end up learning about "trendy" diagnoses such as pathological demand avoidance, oppositional defiant disorder, rejection sensitive dysphoria, and they think, "My son must have one of these extra labels, this can't only be ADHD! There are too many behaviors in the home!"

To make matters more complicated, self-diagnosis has become increasingly normalized in today's world of social media validation. It's not uncommon to come across posts that say things like, "Why spend thousands on a private evaluation when I can just research a diagnosis online, compare the symptoms to my child, and figure it out myself?" The rise in acronyms and layered diagnostic labels—often shared in long, emotional posts—can sometimes reflect the pressure parents feel to make sense of their child's struggles and to be heard in a crowded online space. You might see something like: "Nothing gets through to my AuADHD, high-masking, RSD, ODD, PDA, OCD son—he won't do a single assignment and doesn't care if he fails. He just wants to play Fortnite all day!"

But in reality, all of the behaviors these parents are seeing are related to just one thing: self-regulation. When we understand that ADHD is a disorder of the executive functioning system, there's no need for all of those other labels and acronyms. It's all part of the delay ADHD causes in the development of executive functions.

Self-regulation is the most common symptom—not at school but at home. Yes, the most common ADHD symptoms will be seen at home, around two very specific people: Mom and Dad, the caregivers. The people in the child's life who have one thing that nobody else offers: unconditional love.

The ADHD brain has a hard time comprehending unconditional love. As we will learn, the ADHD brain is rigid, inflexible, and very black and white. There is nothing more fluid, flexible, nuanced, and complex than unconditional love. To the black-and-white ADHD brain, it's much simpler: "Okay, here's this person that I can be at my absolute worst around. I can literally do the opposite of what they tell me to do, I can say 'no' to everything, I can say terrible things to them, and in extreme cases, I can even physically assault them—and you know what I've realized? They will always take care of me! It's not like my classmates at school who choose not to be my friend because of my anger. They love me no matter what! They buy me things, get me any video game I want, buy me the new iPhone, get me my favorite food and snacks, and I do absolutely nothing for them. In fact, I'm incredibly rude and angry toward them! It's amazing!"

Let's point out that this self-talk is, of course, a massive exaggeration. ADHD is not a character flaw. These kids are not malicious. This is just a way to explain the rigidity of their brains and why moms and dads will most often see a whole different child than everyone else gets to see…and it's completely exhausting.

An inability to self-regulate is a major deterrent to personal goals and life success. Dr. Russell Barkley describes this lack of self-regulation and resulting emotional impulsivity as the number-one reason why ADHD kids have such difficulty keeping friendships (ADHD tips 2013, 2:50): "Friends forgive you your distractibility, your forgetfulness, your working memory problems, and even your restlessness. They will not forgive your anger, your hostility, the quickness with which you emote to other people."

While other kids are growing up and learning how to share, involve others, and be mentally flexible, ADHD kids are, on average, 20–45% delayed in self-regulation. So, when you're a fourth grader and your classmates are able to sit through a boring lecture or a difficult assignment, you lack the resiliency to persevere. Your anger gets the best of you. You flip the desk, curse at the teacher, and storm out.

Around this age, kids become much more aware of their social groups and social standings. They don't want to be associated with the angry kid with the short fuse. There are many other cool, calm, and collected peers in the classroom to focus on and interact with. You, the ADHD child, find yourself left out and excluded, due to your inability to manage your emotions.

When I went back to college to get my second bachelor's degree, I had to take classes at night while working full-time. My parents weren't going to pay for another year of college just for me to waste it all again. This time I had to earn my own way. While taking classes at night, I worked at a residential treatment facility (RTF) in New York. There, I met some of the most amazing people I've ever known. People from all sorts of backgrounds, not like the suburban town on Long Island where I grew up. These people knew how to work. They took their jobs and their lives very seriously. At the time, I was very young and immature, but this was the type of job that helped you to grow up, real fast.

We did everything for these kids at the RTF. They lived full-time on the campus, which was also a school. They rarely saw their parents. Basically, the rotating staff was their parents. It was a stressful, heartbreaking, demanding, yet highly rewarding experience.

The hallmark of these children who had to spend their childhood at an RTF was an inability to self-regulate.

They were so easily provoked by each other. Yelling, screaming, cursing, being physically aggressive, trashing their room and the surrounding environments. We had to be trained in-depth on how to restrain a child when safety came into question. Nobody ever wanted to restrain one of these kids. But you learned quickly that it was necessary to keep these children from hurting themselves or others in the heat of the moment.

It was literally like they would flip a switch. Once provoked, they would be a completely different kid. They would go into a full dysregulated rage. In these rages, they would act in ways that didn't align with who they were. They would break their favorite toys, say terrible things to staff members with whom they were very close, and do things they knew would negatively affect their future.

One of my supervisors was a very wise man named Roger. I remember him telling me about his rough upbringing in the Caribbean. He was an amazing worker, leader, and friend. There was another leader named Clint, who sadly passed away during my time working there. He was quite possibly one of the most beloved men I ever met. Everyone respected him. His warming presence instantly put you at ease. He was good at everything and particularly good at bringing others into their talents, helping them to see what they were capable of. I will never forget all that Roger and Clint taught me about these students at the RTF. One quote was incredibly simple yet powerful: "When we are at our angriest, we are at our stupidest."

This is ADHD dysregulation: an inability to internally self-soothe so you externally react in loud, brash, and uncomfortable ways—most often toward those you love the most. When ADHD kids and teens are dysregulated, they make awful decisions. They don't do their schoolwork when they know it will negatively impact them the next day. They don't brush their teeth, shower, or wear clean clothes, knowing they have dealt with bullying from peers because of those choices. They will play video games for 10 hours straight, knowing they have a full checklist of things to do. They will sneak around and lie to their parents, knowing their parents will figure out the truth, punish them, and take away their phone.

It's a vicious cycle of self-sabotage: getting angry, getting "stupid," and losing all rational thinking. These kids aren't able to do the things that actually help them, make them happy, and make them feel successful, all due to the inability to self-regulate.

How Screens Affect Self-Regulation

All of the problems associated with a delay in self-regulation are made worse by screens. We know this from scientific research, and you've probably seen the proof at home or in the classroom, too.

Earlier, we talked about how the ADHD brain handles dopamine differently than a neurotypical brain. That's important when it comes to understanding why screens cause such massive dysregulation in kids and teens with ADHD.

Screen use, especially gaming (Zastrow 2017) and social media (Al-Quran 2022), triggers the release of dopamine. This effect on the brain can lead to addiction, just like an addiction to gambling or drinking alcohol (Griffiths 2018). Like any addict, a child dependent on screens might show withdrawal symptoms such as anxiety, aggression, and irritability when screens are taken away (Bočanová 2024). In short, screens are disrupting the chemical balance of ADHD brains, making it far harder for them to develop and use self-regulation in daily life.

Excessive screen use actually trains the brain to operate in short bursts. As a result, kids who spend lots of time on smartphones are more distractible and less focused

(Qayyum et al. 2024). They struggle to concentrate on extended or nonstimulating tasks. And those are neurotypical kids! For children and teens with ADHD, screens exacerbate their preexisting tendencies and create even more harm.

This is also true in regard to emotional stability, a core aspect of self-regulation. The on-demand world of screens reduces kids' tolerance for frustration, making them emotionally volatile when they don't get the instant results they've learned to expect. Kids become more vulnerable to stress as they struggle to regulate their feelings when confronted with real-life setbacks.

The overstimulation from screens can also increase aggression and rebellious behavior. This often shows up both at school and at home. Specifically, violent media has been shown to have a long-term effect on kids, desensitizing them and causing increased anger and aggression (Bushman and Huesmann 2006).

It's not all about brain chemistry, either. There are several aspects of physical health to consider here as well.

Blue light from screens suppresses melatonin production, disrupting the sleep-wake cycle and preventing deep sleep. With their sleep cycles off-track, kids will be chronically tired and irritable—which will only compound and worsen existing delays in self-regulation and emotional stability. And, as if that wasn't bad enough, extended long-term exposure to artificial blue light has also been linked to cataracts, macular degeneration, and even increased risk for certain types of cancer (Haghani et al. 2024).

The detrimental effects of screens on sleep patterns can also influence emotional well-being. Chronic sleep issues have been shown to affect symptoms of anxiety, depression, and mood disorders (Asarnow and Mirchandaney 2020). Heightened symptoms of these disorders can profoundly worsen overall quality of life—and that's just the opposite of what we want for our kids.

The best thing you can do to help your child develop self-regulation, and all of the other executive functions, is to cut out screens. Unfortunately, that may not be possible when schools provide tablets or laptops as part of the curriculum. And that's a huge problem, for neurotypical students as well as those with ADHD.

I have consulted with more than 500 schools in the past few years. I have heard countless horror stories about school laptops. Cyberbullying has skyrocketed. Teachers have been the target of online attacks (Chang 2024). One major common thing I continue to hear about: students at school, on their school laptops, watching pornography. Absolute insanity. The schools are the ones that gave them every single tool to make that happen.

Someone had the bright idea:

- Let's take the most boring thing in a child's life: a teacher's lesson on an academic topic the student most likely has little to no interest in.
- Let's add the most addicting and stimulating thing possible to this problem: a computer with open access to the Internet.

This is literally like taking a person with a gambling addiction and telling them to go sit in a casino and read a book. You are asking kids to show a level of willpower they simply do not have. We are asking young children and teens to resist the urge to surf the web, play games, or message their friends on a Google Doc—and instead listen to a lecture on Mesopotamia. Yeah, that's totally going to work.

Quite possibly the most common horror story I hear that really scares me is pre-K and kindergarten students doing work on iPads. What are we doing? Why are we all just accepting that this is okay? How are we not jam-packing school board meetings to ensure this never happens in any classroom, ever? Why would little babies need to do educational assessments and tasks on high-tech devices?

These are the young ages when kids need to play and interact with human beings the most. If there is one age group where the dangers of screen time are so incredibly obvious—it's this one. Now we are giving them screens for education? Their brains are not even ready to learn complex things yet. Their brains are not ready for this high level of stimulation.

What school leaders have to realize is that they are basically creating dysregulated kids by doing this. These kids come to school to interact with peers, play, do show and tell, have long recess, sing songs, learn about the weather and the days of the week. Now, we are asking them to do academic tasks on tablets? Giving them a massive rush of dopamine from the stimulus of a swipe of a finger across the glass? This is the definition of insanity.

One important point to note is that every school is different. Some do quite a good job with firewalls and security so that students can't access websites that have nothing to do with what they are learning. But sadly, most schools don't. Most schools have little to no firewall, and if they do have one, the students are better at hacking it than the school's own IT department.

If there was one thing that didn't need to be fixed in America's ever-broken system of education, it was the use of textbooks, paper, pens, pencils, and worksheets.

This is madness. Our most vulnerable population of babies and children is being negatively affected by adult greed. We need laws in place to make sure this ends immediately.

But until we have those laws and leave school laptops behind, we just have to learn how to make the best of a bad situation. Today, with screens and the harm they cause seemingly inescapable, kids with ADHD need our help more than ever.

CHAPTER 7

The Playbook on Self-Regulation

In almost every aspect of life, self-regulation is the make-or-break component. For children, this is especially evident in four areas: self-regulating emotions, self-regulating the body, self-regulating within relationships, and self-regulating the use of technology.

Emotions

"My child gets angry out of nowhere. She'll be fine one second and having a meltdown the next."

"My kid has a hard time thinking before he acts. It's like as soon as he has a strong emotion, his feelings just completely take over."

"My child needs a long time to calm down after an argument or outburst. They're still upset hours after something happened, no matter how minor."

I hear statements like these from parents all the time. And they all come down to the same thing: a lack of self-regulation and, more specifically, a lack of emotional self-regulation.

Both children and adults can experience anger, frustration, boredom, and anxiety that feels overwhelming. As they grow up, kids develop the self-awareness, VWM, and conditional thinking needed to manage their feelings and prevent their emotions from ruling their lives. But because of their delayed executive function, children with ADHD will not be able to keep up with their peers when it comes to regulating their feelings and controlling impulsive, emotion-fueled reactions.

Let's look at an example that shows us what's going on in an ADHD brain during a stressful situation.

In class, a child is starting to become frustrated during a group project because their peers aren't listening to their ideas. First, they'll need the self-awareness to even know when they're getting upset. A child with good self-awareness and a well-developed VWM might recognize how they're feeling and engage in self-talk that helps them cool off: "Maybe if I stay calm, they'll listen to me. I'll try to find a way to combine my ideas with theirs."

But a kid with ADHD won't always recognize a gradual ramp-up of dysregulating emotion. There are no internal "alarm bells" to tell them when their emotions are beginning to spiral out of control. As a result, it may feel like their anger hits out of nowhere.

As soon as that happens, they might struggle to inhibit their initial emotional reaction. Instead of finding a way to compromise or express their feelings, they jump straight to an emotionally charged outburst.

This is directly related to a lack of conditional thinking. Without it, this child with ADHD struggles to anticipate the consequences of their words and actions. They don't have the ability to tell themselves, "If I start shouting and cause a big scene, then my classmates will be upset at me. But if I take a deep breath and calm down, then I'll be able to handle this better." Instead, they respond impulsively, without considering how their uncontrolled reaction might affect the situation.

With no internal checks and balances in place, the student with ADHD erupts in anger with little lead-up or warning. They might abruptly yell over their group mates or lash out and storm away from the table.

Not only are they themselves dysregulated, but now the work on the school project has stalled, their classmates are distracted by the sudden outburst, and the teacher is left trying to wrangle the class's attention back to the task at hand. It's a lose-lose situation for everyone.

Emotional regulation is necessary in all kinds of situations, not just social ones. For instance, when a neurotypical student gets stuck on a complex math problem, they can counter their emerging frustration with their well-developed VWM, telling themselves: "First, I need to multiply, then divide...what was the next step? Let me look back at the example the teacher showed us. This is hard, but I can do it. Let me break it down into smaller steps. I'll figure it out." This emotional self-management allows them to calmly think through various solutions, keeps them motivated, and helps them persevere past obstacles.

But for kids with ADHD, every minor inconvenience can immediately set off dysregulation. Finishing a difficult assignment, dealing with interpersonal conflict, learning an instrument, practicing a new athletic skill—any challenge or setback becomes almost impossible to move past without self-regulation.

Emotional regulation helps us control negative emotions, but it also helps us to behave appropriately when we're feeling strong positive emotions. In a classroom setting, a child might use their self-regulating internal speech to remind themselves: "Okay, I'm excited that I know the answer to the question the teacher is asking, but I need to raise my hand if I want to speak." Without this kind of self-regulation, children will always be interrupting others and speaking out of turn.

So how do we help them develop this ability?

To manage their emotions, kids need to strengthen their "brain coach." Earlier, we discussed some pre-, mid-, and post-task prompts to help kids learn that they have a brain coach and how it can help them. To encourage self-regulation, we can take this a step further by explaining that they have a voice inside their head that they can speak to whenever they are feeling emotional. This voice is always there to help them stay calm, motivated, and regulated.

Many students like to name their brain coach and give it some personality traits. In my clinics, we do role-playing games where we ask students to complete certain tasks while verbally narrating their brain coach so we can hear them talking to themselves. As they strengthen this mental muscle and start using it throughout their day, we are giving them a tool they will use for the rest of their lives.

Once your child is comfortable with their brain coach, you can help them understand how to use it to self-soothe. One great way to do this is to teach them (when they are fully calm at baseline) what "ready" and "not ready" look like.

Make sure to explain this in detail. It might all sound obvious to you as an adult, but kids need you to spell it out with clear and specific expectations: "When you are 'ready,' you are calm, cool, and collected. You do a great job listening. You are able to be your best self. You are able to pause, wait, think, and make very healthy and positive choices. When you are 'not ready,' you are the opposite—you are angry, frustrated, and dysregulated. You are not able to listen to others. You do not stop, think, and make smart choices. During these times, you need to use your brain coach to soothe your thoughts, calm down, and get yourself back to 'ready.'"

Your child should know that when they are "ready," you are there for them. You can talk to them, you can help them, you can engage with them fully. When they are "not ready," you are still there for them, like you always are, but you cannot engage with them. They are upset about something, and they need space to talk with their brain coach about what they are feeling and how they can self-regulate those emotions. When they show that they are "not ready," Mom and Dad need to step away and give them all the time they need to do what they have to do to be "ready" again.

Once they show they are "ready," then, and only then, Mommy and Daddy can talk to them again. Emphasize that they have to *show* they are ready, with their actions, behaviors, language, and volume. They can't just say "I'm ready." Actions speak louder than words.

In classroom settings, it can be helpful to provide students with the means to step back, engage with their brain coach, and bring themselves back to "ready." A good method to do this is with an IEP or 504 accommodation for a predetermined break card system. A "break card" is just what it sounds like—a card that a student can show or place in a designated spot to communicate that they need a break from a specific task or environment. When students are getting frustrated or overwhelmed, they can use their break card, get a pep talk from their brain coach, and then resume what they were doing once they are regulated and calm.

Remember, the main purpose of this accommodation is to help kids develop self-regulation with fading prompts toward independence. The accommodation should state that the break card may be used no more than three times a day. By the end of the year, the student should be permitted to use their break card fewer times per day or receive shorter breaks.

As kids are learning how to use their brain coach to self-soothe, both parents and teachers can help them with affective calmness.

Affective calmness is the ability to stay calm and model calmness in front of a dysregulated child (Wexelblatt 2021). We all know the phrase "misery loves company." This could not be more true about ADHD. ADHD kids and teens use dysregulation to make others dysregulated. When they are angry, bored, or frustrated, seeing a calm, relaxed, composed person is the best medicine. Especially as a parent, this is your role.

Always model self-regulation using affective calmness. Or, at least, aim for "always." But please remember—there is no such thing as a perfect parent. Even the parenting "gurus" you see on social media have terrible days when they make plenty of mistakes. There will be days when you are not your true best self. You will yell, get frustrated, and become dysregulated even when you know you shouldn't. As long as you keep this rule in mind, do your best, and stay calm *most* of the time, you're doing your job.

Contrary to popular belief, your children will not learn emotional regulation skills by listening to your lectures or talking to a talk therapist. They learn by watching us. They learn by seeing us persevere through challenges (Leonard 2024), remaining regulated when they are screaming and trashing the house, and staying calm when the world is falling apart around us.

When your own self-regulation is being tested, you can model your self-talk out loud for them to hear. It is important for kids and teens to know that adults have a brain coach too, and they use it every second of every day! Hearing what a brain coach does for you really helps them to rely on theirs.

Maybe you spill something in the kitchen while you're cooking, or you're getting stressed out when you can't remember where you set your keys. If your kids hear you say, "It's okay. This is frustrating, but I can handle it. I'll stay calm and get back on track," you're giving your child a perfect example of what a brain coach can be.

Body

I've said before that the idea of ADHD kids being "hyper" is a total oversimplification of the disorder. But there's no doubt that hyperactivity is a common and highly visible symptom.

What's important is that we understand hyperactivity as just that: a *symptom*, not the whole disorder. We have to put it into the context of a lack of executive functioning and, specifically, a lack of self-regulation.

Excessive, impulsive movements. Restlessness. Roving around the classroom or school without permission. Endless fidgeting. Struggling to follow directions or wait their turn. Extreme difficulty with any sort of calm, quiet activity. This is what a lack of self-regulation of the body looks like.

This impacts not only kids but also their parents and teachers. Parents might feel embarrassed by their child's antics in public, and they might be exhausted by their seemingly endless supply of energy. They're likely to worry about how their child's behavior will affect their future, and most of all, they feel helpless about how to make things better.

Because our schools are structured around the wildly outdated "lecture-listen" model, where students are expected to sit still for hours on end, teachers often find themselves in an ongoing battle with kids who have ADHD. They might be worn out from having to repeat the same instructions over and over again. They're probably frustrated by the frequent disruptions to lessons, and they may struggle to balance the needs of individual students with ADHD and the needs of their classroom as a whole.

Of course, this isn't malicious on the kids' part. They don't act this way just to annoy the adults around them. In fact, many times, kids wish they didn't have to be so "hyper" and that they could be more like their friends and classmates. When they're constantly in trouble, constantly getting yelled at, and constantly behind their peers, they can start to lose confidence in themselves. They know they're viewed as disruptive and potentially as less capable than other children, which can reinforce a belief that they're just "bad."

But these aren't bad kids. They just need some help developing their self-regulation so that they can thrive alongside their peers.

Earlier, we discussed the fact that kids and teens with ADHD actually need more consequences to help them develop accountability. That's completely true. But there is one thing that should never be used as a bargaining chip and withheld as a consequence: recess.

The days of eliminating recess as a consequence need to end—forever. This is just not appropriate, and there is little to no data to show that it in any way benefits the child or teaches them a skill when they miss out on recess and need to sit alone instead (Beard 2018). Recess is not a privilege, it is a right. It is what all students need and get far too little of. It is already a crime how much recess has declined over the years (Stapp and Karr 2018), and whatever's left is typically fully eliminated after middle school. No, physical education time does not make up for it.

Recess programs need to be expanded across the country and the world. All students, from preschool to twelfth grade, need recess. Screen-free recess, of course. This is especially true for kids with ADHD, who need this movement, free play, and outdoor exercise to soothe their minds and their bodies and get a break from the monotony of the structured school day, away from those bright lights and uncomfortable chairs. For them, movement is not a choice. It's a necessity.

Their brains crave constant stimulation, and physical movement is one way of getting the stimulation their brain needs.

But as we all know, recess and free play are always the first casualty of standardized testing and increased pressure for scores that reflect on school leadership. They need to make themselves look good, so eliminate recess, pressure teachers more to "teach to the test," and force the maximum possible amount of academics on students. All the while, the research tells us that recess, movement, and play actually improve test scores (Hodges et al. 2022; Howie et al. 2023)! Students, even neurotypical ones, who get more free play and recess are more regulated and show more sustained attention toward their schoolwork (Brez and Sheets 2017), and they're more easily able to push themselves through boredom and challenge (Koepp et al. 2022).

Of course, we do have to provide specific support to the child who may present with behaviors that are a safety concern to themselves or others during recess time. In this specific instance, school staff will have to step in and provide services to this child to ensure they are able to participate in this crucial aspect of their day.

In addition to outdoor recess, kids should have plenty of opportunities to get out from behind their desks and move their bodies throughout the day. Ideally, for younger kids, movement breaks should take place every 20–30 minutes.

Teachers, you can get creative with this. Create a deck of laminated cards with one- to two-minute activities. Draw cards at random, or let kids take turns picking their favorites. To help you brainstorm, here are some quick and easy movement breaks:

- Do wall push-ups for one minute.
- Do chair stretches for two minutes.
- Walk like an animal (bear crawl, crab walk).
- Follow along with GoNoodle or Just Dance videos.

- Do 10 jumping jacks.
- Touch four corners of the room.
- March in place for 30 seconds.

These don't have to be teacher-led activities, either. Kids with ADHD are great at moving! So whenever possible, let them lead a movement break.

Teachers can also assign various classroom tasks that include movement. For example, they can give out roles like "paper passer," "whiteboard cleaner," and "mail deliverer" so that students are moving around in a way that's helpful rather than disruptive. These tasks allow them to contribute to the classroom and feel valued while also making it easier for them to self-regulate once they return to their seat.

Inevitably, even with all of these strategies, there will still be times when redirection is needed. Teachers, be intentional about how you do this. Rather than just scolding a child for disobeying, use "check-in tools" that encourage self-awareness and self-regulation. If a student is out of their seat when they're supposed to be at their desk, you can use prompts like "Where is your body right now?"

Model self-talk that will help students acknowledge and regulate where they are, what they're doing, and how their body should look. For example, you can teach self-regulatory internal phrases like "Feet on the floor, eyes on my paper" and "I can wiggle my fingers but stay in my seat."

Most importantly, increase recess, and increase movement breaks. Our students need them. This is vital for limiting impulsive movements but also for developing self-regulation and executive functions in general.

Relationships

Parents, sometimes it can seem like your child with ADHD is out to antagonize you every chance they get. You're not imagining it: your ADHD child has a brain that seeks negative attention.

This is a concept that is so incredibly important for parents to understand. Kids with ADHD get a dopamine tsunami when they are told they are doing something wrong, inappropriate, rude, or bad. The same kind of dopamine tsunami they get when they play a video game. The ADHD brain would rather hear "no, don't do that" than "good job, I am proud of you!" Your child's brain *wants* that negative feedback (Amen 2020).

The ADHD brain will seek out center stage. It wants to hold the microphone and have the spotlight. Kids with this type of neurodiverse brain want all the attention they can get, for as long as possible. They are driven by the power trip of having their entire family, and their emotional state, in the palm of their hand.

What's the easiest way to get that power? Do something that you know your parents cannot ignore and need to provide instant negative feedback to. Mom is no longer reading her book; Dad is no longer doing the laundry. They've dropped everything and put all of their focus, attention, and energy on me.

These kids may be crying, screaming, cursing at their parents, and using self-defeating comments that are hard to hear—but the truth is, their brain is stimulated when they feel a sense of control over their parents, even when they are being verbally reprimanded. Other children may receive feel-good messages from their brain when they earn praise and affirmations. They can self-regulate in their relationships with parents, teachers, and siblings to seek positive interactions and avoid conflict. But for kids with ADHD, their brains are wired to do just the opposite. Their brains are conflict-seeking. This is not attention-deficit disorder; this is negative-attention-stimulation disorder.

This is especially true when the ADHD child or teen leaves baseline and becomes dysregulated. And as we've already learned, emotional self-regulation is a constant challenge for these kids.

If you have a child with ADHD who recognizes that it is easy to push your buttons, so simple to make you emotional, a quick task to get you dysregulated—you are in trouble. That sense of control over your emotions will drive their behavior and open the floodgates for dopamine.

I always have to add context to this information by saying that ADHD is not a character flaw. They are not being malicious. They are not sociopaths. They are simply doing what works and what feels good. That does not make them a bad person. It makes them a neurodiverse child with a unique brain. Because of this constant negative attention seeking, parents often find themselves in a very toxic relationship with their ADHD child. My good friend and *ADHD Parenting Podcast* co-host Ryan Wexelblatt coined the phrase "the argument vortex" and discusses it in depth in his online parent training programs (Wexelblatt 2025). There is no better phrase to define where ADHD parents find themselves every single day. Stuck in the vicious vortex.

There are three specific times of the day when parents are most susceptible to getting sucked into the vortex: the morning routine before school, the after-school homework routine, and the bedtime routine.

Why these three specific experiences? These are three times when parents tend to interject themselves too deeply into what the child is doing. This is the "ADHD Parenting Paradox": having a child who is highly prompt dependent and needs constant prompts and reminders to get tasks done and is also highly stimulated by negative attention and uses it against the parents to create further dysregulation and arguments.

To some extent, all children are prompt dependent and require their parents to act as their executive function system. But for our ADHD kids, this is taken to a whole new extreme. They need the prompts, but when you prompt them, it turns into a massive fight, every single time. This is where much of the exhaustion and stress of ADHD parenting comes from.

During the morning routine, parents, especially mothers, feel like they have to prompt their child 100 times for them to get ready for school on time. They may follow the child around the house, reminding them of every little step they must take. Get dressed, brush your teeth, eat your breakfast, put your shoes on. None of those things will happen without full maximum verbal prompting and warnings.

The reality is that the child is loving the prompts and attention, and they feel incredibly powerful when they are able to pull their parents into the vortex before school. It makes their morning engaging and fun. They are no longer going through a boring and tedious routine; they now have entertainment—their stressed and dysregulated mother following them around all morning.

Homework is another time when parents are in danger of losing themselves in the vortex. Often, parents will be filled with anxiety when they know there are only a few minutes left before their child is going to come walking in that door after school. Why? Because once they get home, they might argue with parents for three straight hours over 10 minutes of homework. The whole time, the child is absolutely loving this game of cat and mouse. They feel a sense of control as they know exactly what to do to evoke a deep emotional response in their parent, while at the same time avoiding the boring and nonstimulating task of homework.

And the same thing happens when it's time to put on pajamas and get ready for bed. While parents attempt to micromanage the bedtime routine, their kids with ADHD are getting an infusion of dopamine every time they hear the prompts, lectures, and reprimands. The parents think they are helping, but when it comes to the ADHD brain, this could not be more wrong.

All of these instinctual choices are made by parents simply trying to do their best and get to the end of the day as a healthy and happy family. Going off your instincts may work with a neurotypical child, but we have to remember, this is no typical and ordinary child we're talking about. This is a child with ADHD and a conflict-seeking brain.

The endless prompting and overinvolvement are actually inhibiting the child's attainment of executive functioning. It is keeping the child highly dependent on the negative stimulation and preventing them from developing the skills to self-regulate their emotions, routines, and relationships in healthy ways.

Parents often get very caught up in consequences. How can I best punish my child or give them the appropriate consequence for refusing to cooperate and provoking arguments every chance they get? Consequences have their place. But oftentimes, grounding your child, making them sit in their room, having them lose privileges, or making them miss out on things just won't work and will not teach any skill. As we discussed earlier, these kids cannot connect the dots between their actions and the punishment. We have to get out of the mindset of using punishments to change this behavior.

Here is what you need to do instead: ignore them. Losing your attention, or never getting it in the first place, is the best possible consequence.

What they need is a detox. Any response they get to their negative behavior will provide that dopamine rush, and it will unintentionally reinforce the behavior. But when we detox from negative stimulation, we retrain their brains to show them that those behaviors don't work anymore. Doing the wrong things for shock value is not going to get them what they're looking for. When you ignore, walk away, and do not respond to their attention-seeking behavior, you are teaching them that negative actions will not provide a dopamine reward, and that there are better ways to get Mom and Dad's attention.

It should come as no surprise that this is one of the most difficult evidence-based strategies for parents to actually follow. I am sure many of you are thinking: "I've tried to ignore her, but she will just follow me around and not stop until I engage!" Yes, at first, you can expect your child to go around the house looking for stimulation in the form of negative attention from Mom, Dad, and their siblings. They will prod and poke every single button they can to ensure they are the center of attention.

We already talked about the importance of teaching your child what "ready" looks like: calm, at baseline, and acting as their best self. As you work through the detox, do whatever you need to do to ensure you are only engaging with your child when they are "ready." You are going to become a master at ignoring. You can lock yourself in the bathroom, leave the house, or tag in your partner. Of course, safety is always the number-one priority, so make sure your child is out of harm's way while you are not engaging with them.

It can be difficult for parents to stay regulated while their child is doing everything in their power to provoke a reaction. That's exactly why practicing self-care is so incredibly important for all parents, especially those with ADHD themselves. We know that ADHD is a hereditary disorder, so there is a high probability that one or both parents have ADHD as well. All parents, but particularly parents with ADHD, need to ensure they have plenty of outlets and hobbies that refocus their attention and provide healthy stimulation outside of their children: meditation, exercise, going on walks, listening to podcasts—whatever works for you.

Understand that this process is not going to be successful immediately. It is going to take time to detox your child's brain from the negative attention stimulation. But once you've done this, your child will finally be able to develop the internal self-regulation they need to get through their day without seeking conflict at every turn. It's hard, but you can do this.

Technology

One of the worst things to ever happen to education is personal laptops for each student.

For all those parents who fought the fight and did what they had to do to remove screens in the house, schools made things even harder on them with a personal laptop that has to come home every day for homework, projects, and studying. These laptops come in all shapes, sizes, and models. Some schools give out tablets, others full computer laptops. Some are hunky and clunky, others are shiny and chic. But one thing they have in common—they are a total disaster.

When students use laptops during lectures, 38 minutes out of every 60 minutes are spent off-task (Ragan et al. 2014). This right here is all the information we need to know that school laptops are a massive failure. Kids—ADHD and neurotypical—simply cannot self-regulate around them. They cannot resist the urge to be off-task doing fun, engaging, more stimulating things instead of listening to boring lectures. The laptops are possibly good in theory, but not according to science and child development.

Even students themselves know this. I've worked with numerous students who told me every time I saw them how much they hated their school laptop, but they just could not stop themselves from going on it for multiple hours a day every day. It's a drug, they know it, and they know they can't stop themselves.

Too often, when parents bring up their concerns about the rampant misuse of laptops, schools wave the white flag: "Sorry, we can't do anything about that. We monitor what websites they are going on, but we cannot block anything. We need them to learn to do the right thing on the computer and learn to resist the urge to go on noneducational websites." What is going on here? What world are we living in? We expect kids to be able to "resist the urge"? They're children! Stuck at boring school with a computer sitting in front of them. They are humans, not robots. Even adults at work surf the web and go on their phones when they get bored. For a child, of course it is going to be far more frequent and far worse.

The biggest problem is what these laptops are keeping children from experiencing. They are keeping them indoors, sedentary, and stuck on instant gratification. They are keeping them away from going outside, walking, moving, riding bikes, climbing trees, participating in sports, singing, dancing, and playing in-person with peers. This is incredibly dangerous. Not only are laptops an overwhelming obstacle to self-regulation, but they also hold kids back from the experiences that allow them to develop stronger executive functions in general.

The good news is that people are starting to push back. Parents everywhere are telling their school leadership to ditch the laptops. And if the schools don't want to cooperate, parents do legally have the right to opt out. They do not have to participate in this sick and twisted science experiment. They can have their student go back to pen and paper.

When schools hear parents request this, they do everything they can to distract and avoid. They don't want to put more work on the shoulders of the teachers, and of course this is understandable. They don't want teachers to cater to all the students with laptops and then have to create different materials for the few children without one.

But we can't let the schools deter us. We need parents to get louder and louder. We need them to use strength in numbers, go to all the school board meetings, and demand an end to EdTech. We can go back to the days of computer labs in schools where kids have one class a day on the computer to learn appropriate research and other tasks such as using Microsoft Word and PowerPoint. Do they need constant exposure to technology so they can be ready for the job market? Absolutely not. That is a false cognitive distortion. What they need is outdoor play to develop executive skills needed for work, life, and everything.

Until then, until school laptops are gone for good, there is only one solution. You, the parent, need to take control over that school laptop. No more free ownership and unlimited use that leads to full-on addiction. This is your house, your rules. Your child's overall health and acquisition of skills for their future is your goal and your responsibility as a parent. This Chromebook can no longer own your child's brain.

Here is what you will do moving forward: You will set a designated hour for your child to do homework. For example, maybe they get home from school at 3 p.m. You let them relax and decompress in nonscreen ways until 3:30. Then, the hour of 3:30–4:30 is the hour they get to do homework with their school laptop.

I know what many of you are thinking—one hour? That's it? My child will need more like three or four. First of all, there is little to no research that doing more than one hour of homework is beneficial to a child or teen. It will not help with information retention, will not improve their grades, and will certainly not make them more engaged in their learning (Kohn 2006). If they consistently receive one hour of work time, the child will eventually learn to take their hour very seriously and not go on YouTube during homework time.

When that hour is over, the laptop goes back to you—no ifs, ands, or buts. It does not matter if the child says they need more time or not. Too bad. They should have been more productive during that hour.

If they truly didn't finish their homework, that is a school problem, not a home problem. The teacher will have to hold them accountable for not having their work completed.

You keep the laptop (hopefully under lock and key) until the next morning when the child leaves to go back to school.

Implementing this might sound difficult, and honestly? It is. But all good things take time. We have to persevere through the struggle and the discomfort to give our kids a fighting chance to develop the self-regulation skills they need.

PART III

Self-Motivation

CHAPTER 8

The Third Pillar

Everything Is Nonpreferred

Meet Dylan. He is 11 years old, and has a variety of interests and hobbies. However, due to his delayed executive functioning, he struggles to find the self-motivation for anything that isn't exciting or interesting to him. For Dylan and his parents, this creates daily problems with homework and chores.

His parents frequently hear from his teachers that he is a very capable student, but he rarely completes assignments on time, or at all. When he's at home, his mom tries to give him gentle reminders about his schoolwork, but he always protests that he'll "do it later."

The idea of focusing on schoolwork feels overwhelming to him, and without immediate rewards, he struggles to find the motivation to begin. Even though Dylan knows there will be consequences to not doing his assignments, like getting a poor grade or being told off by the teacher, he still has a hard time getting started. When his mom tries to put her foot down, Dylan's frustration escalates rapidly. His lack of self-regulation makes it difficult to calm down, and his spiraling, out-of-control emotions result in yelling, tantrums, and, of course, further delays in starting his homework.

Dylan's parents have tried using rewards as well as consequences. They've promised extra screen time if he finishes his homework and taken away his favorite games when he doesn't. These external motivators might be effective—but only temporarily, while his parents are there to remind him to stay on task. The moment they're not, he loses focus and abandons his work.

Dylan's lack of self-motivation isn't confined to school assignments. On weekends, for example, his parents ask him to do chores around the house, like taking out the trash. No matter how small the task is, he puts off doing it, claiming he'll get to it later. Hours pass, and his chores remain untouched until his parents intervene.

It's the same story when it comes to extracurricular activities. Dylan loves playing soccer. But when his team has a game or a practice, he has difficulty motivating himself to pack his gear and get to the field on time without someone else prompting him repeatedly.

Even meetups with friends become a challenge. He might want to go hang out with a friend, but if the process of leaving the house feels too overwhelming, he might struggle to find the motivation to get ready. Ultimately, he may refuse to go altogether. In the end, Dylan misses out on good grades, healthy physical activity, and vital social relationships, all due to his inability to self-motivate.

Self-Motivation in a World of Instant Gratification

When I am doing my GrowNOW intake calls with parents, if there is one thing I discuss that most often prompts the parent to say "Yup, that's my kid," it's this: self-motivation.

Before our calls, many parents are confused by this concept of self-motivation. They will start out by saying things like "There is no way my son has issues with self-motivation; he can play Minecraft for 10 hours straight!" I'll have to explain that, well, yeah, of course he can. That's an addictive video game. That's his comfort zone. That is a top-tier preferred task. And that's when it clicks for parents.

When we discuss self-motivation as an executive function skill, we have to remember that it is about nonpreferred tasks. That's the focus—the ability to motivate yourself toward tasks that are not instantly gratifying like a video game or a smartphone app. Do you have the ability to motivate yourself toward something new, boring, challenging?

This is a crucial skill in life, and it is something that is absolutely necessary for success. Why? Because most tasks we need to do in life are nonpreferred and not instantly gratifying. Most of us do not really want to go grocery shopping, pay the bills, exercise, shower, brush our teeth, prepare healthy meals, or even go to work. But we have to, regardless of our diagnosis. We have to do these things to stay healthy, to not be reliant on others, and to live our best lives.

So why do parents identify so emotionally and so deeply with this issue of kids' self-motivation? Because the world in which kids are growing up today is a world of instant gratification. There are no longer abundant opportunities for boredom, problem-solving, critical thinking, and free play (Singer et al. 2009; Mullan 2019). Screens, Google, GPS, and video games have replaced our need to organically practice these skills. Kids' brains are becoming hardwired toward instant gratification (Richardson et al. 2024).

It's well-documented that too much screen time can lead to extreme challenges with patience and perseverance, making it difficult for kids and teens to set and achieve goals that require sustained effort. This is especially true for kids who use fast-paced social media, which interferes with the ability to delay gratification (Sriram 2023).

Real-life activities just can't compete with digital stimulation. When a child's world shrinks down to a screen, it inevitably leads to a loss of hobbies, learning opportunities, and varied life experiences.

If screens are available, there is no need to focus on what's to come in the future anymore; the present is too gratifying. "What is in front of me is all I need. The world around me is unnecessary when I have my phone that will pull me away from boredom."

For parents, this is where the burnout starts. Getting your child off their phone or away from their games to do even the most basic task is like pulling teeth. "But how do I get my child to just do that task?" might be the question I receive most frequently from parents. The lack of internal self-motivation is the core issue.

Academics: Reading, Writing, and Homework

Self-motivation is necessary for us to accomplish any task that's tough, boring, or not immediately rewarding. For many kids, that includes anything to do with academics.

There are two specific academic tasks that students with ADHD often struggle with: written expression and reading comprehension. These are the students who end up staring at a blank Google Doc all class period instead of writing a sentence. They will also have to read the same paragraph four to five times to fully understand it.

This is because these two specific tasks require the greatest amount of self-motivation and executive functioning. As we learned earlier, all executive functioning starts with nonverbal working memory and the visual imagery system. Ideally, you are starting to connect the dots here.

There is no success in reading and writing without strong executive functions.

One of the best ways to understand what executive functioning truly is is to look at it as internal play. The brain plays with thoughts, ideas, distractions, the past, the present, the future, plans, problems, and stress, all at once. It is playing with all of these things at any given moment. Play is not just something for little kids at the playground or in the sandbox. Play never stops. Executive functioning is play.

Well, so is reading. Reading is the ability to play with information in your mind while continuing to read. Reading is also multitasking, another thing individuals with ADHD struggle with.

Does all this mean that individuals with ADHD just shouldn't have to read because their brains are not built for it? Absolutely not! If anything, they should be reading more than neurotypical people. They just need some additional help and guidance to be successful. A very high percentage of all academics involve literacy, close to 100%. When a student gains confidence in their ability to read and write, they are prepared to succeed in science, math (Akbasli et al. 2016), history (Ozensoy 2021), and various electives.

Because of their struggles with self-motivation, kids with ADHD need extra support so they can accomplish their academic goals. One thing that's going to set them back more than it's ever going to help them? Screens. Screen use is associated with reduced classroom engagement and academic success, particularly in math (Pagani et al. 2010) and language skills (Madigan et al. 2020). It's scary but true: overuse of screens can even contribute directly to reduced cognitive abilities and stunted intellectual growth (Presta et al. 2024).

A few hours after school spent on YouTube and video games will make it a lot harder for your child to pay attention, focus, read, write, and persevere through nonstimulating academic tasks. Not to mention, it will be that much more challenging for your child to self-motivate toward reading and writing when they know the games are just sitting there in another room waiting to be played. You also don't want them playing games after their schoolwork, because they will get so entranced and dysregulated by the game that they risk not retaining what they studied. It will also be difficult for them to get a good night's sleep after being dysregulated by screens.

We cannot afford to let these kids who are already struggling fall any further behind. Parents, once again: face your fears, get these screens out of the house, persevere through the withdrawal behaviors, and build that positive structure in your home to support your child's well-being, as well as your own.

While there's plenty that parents can do to support kids with reading and writing, schools are the other piece of the puzzle. Unfortunately, the typical accommodations you see for ADHD students in schools simply do not help, as most teachers and school staff are not specifically trained in ADHD and executive functioning. In many cases, the default accommodation for ADHD students is the use of a graphic organizer. Like most accommodations used in schools, these organizers are great in theory but not so great in actual practice. Graphic organizers are often teacher-created, so the student does not feel a personalized sense of ownership and creative control over the tool. There are better, evidence-based accommodations that we can implement to actually help students.

With both the writing and reading process, there is a step that schools often miss: students' emotions toward these activities. We need to ensure that reading and writing are not seen as boring or daunting tasks that they want to stay away from for the rest of their lives. Reading in particular is highly correlated to success in school and life, and it is an art and a skill that we cannot allow to be lost in this technological era.

One reason that homework is such a significant challenge for kids with ADHD is that almost all homework involves some amount of reading or writing. But another reason that children, both neurotypical and those with ADHD, may struggle with homework is that we are simply asking too much of them.

Teachers are under a lot of pressure to ensure that students are learning the curriculum so they can perform well on standardized tests. It is a common mindset that if the child reviews class material and practices at home, they will better retain the information. In so many ways, this belief is inaccurate (Kohn 2006). There is little research backing up homework for elementary or even middle school students. Doing schoolwork at home often does not lead to better information retention or higher test scores.

With all that said, homework is unavoidable. In a perfect world, schools would follow the wealth of research and let kids play outside all day after school. But this is the American education system. As we all know, we don't follow research. We follow test scores and profit. Homework is something that you should not expect to go away anytime soon. All we can do for now is help students make the most of an imperfect system.

The Myth of "Masking" and Screens as Motivation

It is far more common for a child with ADHD to struggle at home than at school. Why is that? School is structured, and home is unstructured. School has clear-cut rules that are black and white and easy to understand. School has peers around to model behaviors and increase positive social expectations. Kids don't want to embarrass themselves in front of their peers.

Home could not be more different. Home has something school could never have: unconditional love. And that unconditional love sometimes leads parents to make decisions that they believe are helpful for their kids but, in reality, are causing more harm than good.

Social media tells parents that students with ADHD will "mask" all day by holding in their ADHD behaviors to appear neurotypical. Then, when they get home, they are absolutely exhausted from "masking" for hours. According to this belief, kids "use up" all their self-motivation to behave appropriately while in school and have none left to do homework or other tasks required of them at home. This idea of "masking" became popular and spread around social media by "lived experience" influencers.

Social media has allowed regular everyday people, with no true training in a specific area, to pose as experts. In the neurodiverse world, they are able to dispel this problem by emphasizing the importance of "lived experience." I totally understand the benefits of lived experience and the comfort level it can provide, knowing that you are hearing from someone who has some similarities with your child. However, lived experience does not discount science, research, and evidence-based practices.

This idea that children mask all day and then let loose at home is music to the ears of the permissive parent. "Oh, it can't be anything I do! It's not that I do not set boundaries or limits or that I give them unlimited screen time. They're just exhausted from their masking!"

Doing well at school but not at home is not "masking"; it's commonplace. This idea of masking does not give children the credit they deserve. They respond well to the structure, accountability, and varied relationships at school. Let's not discount their hard work by calling it "masking."

When parents buy into the "masking" idea and remain permissive, they are moving further away from creating the structured environment that allows kids with ADHD to thrive. Simply put, the concept of masking allows parents to avoid holding kids accountable. They protect them from facing the consequences of their actions, believing that the child is simply too tired to do any better. But this is deeply unfair to the child.

Experiencing negative emotions is exactly how children develop self-motivation skills. For example, they will learn to try harder at sports when they realize other players are better and more competent or getting more playing time than them, and they don't like the way that feels. When parents say, "No, you don't have to go to practice," and "Yes, it's fine if you quit the team that you made a commitment to," kids will never have the opportunity to experience that negative emotion or to develop those motivational skills.

So how do you motivate your child toward a task? Some methods are better than others. Often, parents go about this in a way that's just not sustainable in the long term.

To encourage kids to do basic tasks at home, many parents will try various forms of rewards as a replacement for internal self-motivation. Children can be motivated by rewards suited to their developmental stage. For younger kids, stickers, candy, toys, and ice cream will do the trick. This is usually not too difficult for parents to navigate. But once you've set that precedent, then what happens? Once we hit the preteen years, things become more stressful. Around this time, kids' interests become more extensive and expensive. You are no longer getting a packet of stickers for less than a dollar: you now have to go buy a $500 video game system, controllers, and an online gaming subscription.

The largest conundrum here is that around this time, we expect our kids to become more internally self-motivated.

We as parents get tired of buying rewards that our kids become obsessed with, overuse, and fight with us about. But this is what motivates them: video games and new smartphones. The exact things that are keeping them from developing the crucial executive function of self-motivation.

This leads me to one of the most common, most destructive myths that parents believe. I hear it all the time from families: "Screen time encourages good behavior. It's the only thing I can use to motivate him. Without screen time, I cannot get him to shower, brush his teeth, finish homework, or do anything nonpreferred." Parents will often tell me this as if it is a positive thing: "All I have to do is threaten his screen time or present it as a reward and he instantly gets motivated and does what he needs to do." No, this is absolutely a losing proposition.

Kids and teens were not made to have a highly addictive carrot dangling over their heads at all times. This is not a good situation for parents to be in, and something they need to analyze about themselves quickly. If you are reading this right now and you believe this is describing you and your parenting style—if each day you are threatening screen time and using it as a carrot to get your child to do basic tasks—you need to take a step back and realize the hole you are digging yourself into. You don't motivate an alcoholic by letting them know they can have a sip of alcohol if they do a challenging task.

You are creating an environment in which your child is not going to be able to develop true self-motivation skills. We don't want to send them off to college with no IEP, no 504, and no constant parental assistance, after they've spent their entire life getting all of their motivation from the carrot of screen time. There will be absolutely nothing stopping them from playing video games or scrolling on their phone day and night. What will happen to them then?

Parents, you do not want to get stuck in this back-and-forth of using screen time as a tool for motivation. If you find yourself in this hole, you have even more reason to fully eliminate screens, stay strong through the withdrawal behaviors, and take the time to rewire your child's brain so they can be motivated by emotions and experiences. I brush my teeth and I take a shower, simply because I like how I feel when I am done. It also gives me confidence socially when engaging with others, knowing my hygiene is taken care of. I study for tests because I know that when I do, I get a good grade, and I like how that feels. I get ready on time in the morning, because when I am late and I miss the bus, I don't like how that feels. This is true self-motivation. This is what kids need, not the carrot.

A lack of self-motivation creates a daily battle for parents. As adults, we know that there are places to go, tasks to be done, and promises to be kept. But having a child with ADHD throws all of this into disarray. You are now on ADHD time, consistently late. It becomes necessary for you to act as the executive functioning for your child. The absence of self-motivation causes the child to be on their own time, not taking into account the thoughts and feelings of others, not understanding how their lack of urgency deeply affects their loved ones.

We can help our kids do better.

CHAPTER 9

The Playbook on Self-Motivation

Self-motivation is at the core of so many of the most common problems for kids with ADHD. As a parent or a teacher, you're likely to see that these children are unable to self-motivate toward daily routines, homework, reading and writing tasks, studying, and self-improvement.

Daily Routines

The routines and rituals to get ready for the day or wind down for the night may come easily to some kids. But not kids with ADHD.

We've seen how a variety of factors converge to make home routines particularly challenging for kids with ADHD. Successfully maintaining a routine requires a ton of conditional thinking, NVWM-powered foresight, and a good understanding of consequences in order to take all the necessary steps and prevent negative outcomes. And, of course, it also requires a huge amount of internal self-motivation to avoid distractions and stick to necessary routines—even when they're boring, nonstimulating, and repetitive.

In the previous chapter, I talked about how "protecting" kids from negative outcomes and experiences is really just shielding them from developing self-motivation. The morning routine gives us a perfect example.

Kids are not going to develop the self-motivation to keep up with their morning routine without first experiencing what happens when they don't. They need to know what it feels like to be late. How crappy it feels to walk into the main office, sign in, and explain why they're tardy. When they get to class and open the door, their peers are already sitting down at their desks, and they all turn their heads and look over at them. That's not a good feeling. This negative feeling will help them to gain internal self-motivation and finally stop being so prompt dependent on Mom and Dad.

We have to allow the child to experience discomfort. If we shield them from discomfort, we pull away the opportunities for them to develop this crucial set of skills they so badly need.

I am sure many of you have some thoughts about this plan. If your first thought is "Isn't this creating unnecessary trauma and ADHD shame?"—no, it isn't. That is mostly social media pseudoscience nonsense. Everyone has been late to something at some point in their life. It is not traumatic; it is temporary discomfort. Temporary discomfort is how we all develop skills.

But as we allow kids to experience discomfort, we also need to offer them the tools to improve their abilities to self-monitor and self-motivate.

Here is an effective strategy I learned from the great Sarah Ward of Cognitive Connections. It involves the implementation of real-world photos to provide students with the visual image of what they are supposed to look like during different tasks (Ward and Jacobsen 2014). This helps to aid their deficit in NVWM and future thinking. Instead of a verbal prompt or a written checklist, we provide the student with a picture of what we expect of them.

An important point to note is that you have to get a real-world image of that child doing the exact task or behavior you need them to do, in the exact place where they are expected to do it. This will not be effective if you use Google Images and provide a visual prompt of a totally different child in a totally different place.

You can take a picture of your child brushing their teeth, packing their backpack, putting on their shoes, and any other steps you expect them to complete as part of their home routines.

This strategy also has many other potential applications. For example, it could be used for:

- A student who has difficulty sitting during circle time
- A student who uses their school laptop inappropriately
- A student who does not play nicely with others and often gets dysregulated by them
- A student who does not clean up after themself
- A student who forgets to turn work in after completing it
- A student who often forgets materials needed for class

We need to ignite two things with this strategy—NVWM and mirror neurons. Through mirror neurons, we can see another person's action, and that activates our own neurons as if we ourselves are taking the action (Rizzolatti and Sinigaglia 2016). This offers a way to jump-start NVWM and future thinking, paving the way for self-motivation. The child sees themself doing what is expected of them and knows what they are supposed to look like. For a child or teen, especially one with ADHD and conflict-seeking behaviors, this will be far more effective than anything verbal. Language makes dysregulation worse—and it will always be more stimulating to do the opposite of a verbal prompt. With a visual, it's short, sweet, and to the point. The child is provided the visual and competes with themselves to make their body look like it does in the image.

Homework

We know ADHD is a disorder of the executive functioning system and the lack of the ability to self-regulate and self-motivate toward nonpreferred, nonstimulating, and challenging tasks. Unfortunately, to the child or teen, those three adjectives describe about 90% of schoolwork. Taking notes, studying, doing math, reading, and writing do not offer instant gratification and will become strongly nonpreferred by the ADHD student the more they experience struggle and negativity around it.

Kids with ADHD might get an assignment with a deadline that's days or weeks away. And if you're reading this book, then you already know the rest of the story. Instead of thinking "If I do a little bit each day, then I'll be done on time," they don't even get started until the last possible moment. The whole household ends up affected by the resulting stress and frustration. The work either gets done in a rush and earns a low grade, or it just never gets turned in at all.

This can be especially hard for parents and teachers to see, because not doing homework doesn't mean that children aren't intelligent or capable. These kids might be very bright, but their inability to self-motivate creates a cycle of underachievement. No matter what parents say or do to persuade their kids to get their schoolwork done on time, the self-motivation just isn't there.

Homework is a major anxiety producer for parents. But it does not have to be.

Remember, homework is one of the three most common times for the argument vortex. Parents tend to get overly involved, try to micromanage, and end up stimulating their child with negative attention. So first things first—you are the parent, not the homework secretary. It takes a lot of willpower and strength for parents to stop being so over-involved with homework. Let's be honest, this is especially true for moms. Many moms seem to have made it their mission to ensure homework is done correctly and efficiently each and every day under their direct supervision. In all my years of working with ADHD students and families, I have never once seen this method benefit a child and their parents. All I have ever seen this do is absolutely toxify their relationship and lead to huge daily fights, causing the child to end up hating homework even more.

Let's face the facts. You need to find the inner strength to stop micromanaging your child's academic performance. As long as you remain involved, you are making it too easy for your child to start arguments instead of actually doing their work. They have a conflict-seeking brain. They want the fighting, the arguing, the yelling, and that strong sense of control over you and your emotions. If there is a yelling match happening instead of them doing their homework—you are playing right into their game, and they are winning. No, this is not a character flaw. No, they are not malicious. They are simply doing what works and what stimulates their brain.

You need to back off. You need to back off completely. You are their mom, not their teacher. Your presence is making homework an overwhelmingly negative experience for your child.

Next, we have to change the environment. Homework should not be done at home. Homework should be done away from the home, away from the negative interactions with parents and away from distracting and dysregulating screens. This is especially true for ADHD students. If you ever lived in a college dorm, you probably remember needing to get away from your roommates and go to the library for a few hours to get your work done. This is that same mindset. We need to create that structure for our kids and teens.

Find a location that works for your child and your family—at a local library or YMCA, or with a peer. The absolute best place for kids to do homework is at school, because that's where the homework comes from and that's what it's for.

If your school offers a "homework club" or any other opportunities for your child to do homework at school, do it. This has two benefits. First, students will not have the temptations and distractions of home. Second, if homework is done at school, there will most likely be teachers and other educational professionals there to assist them. This is much better than your typical parents experiencing headaches while they try to remember seventh-grade math.

And guess what? This is not your child's choice—it's yours. You're the parent; you're the adult. You don't ask your child if they want to do homework club, you sign them up yourself because you know it's best for them. You contact the school and ensure your child is participating. They are not to get on the bus, and you do not pick them up until after homework club is completed. Someday, they will thank you for the grit, self-motivation, and frustration tolerance they developed from this experience.

Reading and Writing

Writing is particularly difficult for students with ADHD. This is because writing is unbelievably slow. It is a meticulous process that requires an extensive amount of planning and internal organization to have the information travel from your brain, down your arm, and to your hand where you will write or type.

This task requires an absolute ton of self-regulation, self-motivation, and frustration tolerance. Nothing about writing is instantly gratifying. In fact, it's quite the opposite. The writing process offers no gratification until days, or sometimes even weeks, later. The arduous back-and-forth revision process until you have a final product is the definition of delayed gratification. The ADHD brain has a hard time handling that.

Reading comprehension is also quite difficult for individuals with ADHD, for many of the same reasons as written expression. The biggest reason, of course, is the visual imagery provided by the NVWM that is needed to read. If you are not visualizing what you are reading, then what are you really even doing anyway? You will quickly get bored and agitated, give up, and go do something more stimulating.

Reading relies on self-regulation, self-motivation, and, of course, the ability to delay gratification. This is why in today's world of screens and instant gratification, so few people read or are able to read. According to 2023 data, out of 31 countries, the United States is tied for 14th in literacy skills (National Center for Education Statistics 2024).

Additionally, reading requires an extensive amount of mental flexibility. Instead of writing your own story, you are reading someone else's and following their lead. You are taking their direction and their characters and story and creating your own individualized interpretation of it. Of course, for the ADHD brain, this is all quite difficult. And if reading and writing are difficult, most other academic tasks will be too.

No matter how much AI and ChatGPT become a way of life in the future, the skills of reading and writing will absolutely still be in demand and will always improve an individual's quality of life. These are two important skills that must be developed by the time an individual graduates from high school. The current rate of high school students having to drop out because they are unable to effectively read or write is becoming highly concerning (Carlson 2010). There is no doubt that Big Tech and their addictive products, as well as our school system (not our teachers), are to blame.

But kids with ADHD absolutely can develop their self-motivation toward reading and writing, as long as they have the right strategies and accommodations to support them.

> My personal favorite strategy for helping students to effectively and successfully write is to follow these steps:
>
> 1. Have the student talk about what they want to write. Ask them to tell the story out loud.
> 2. Once they have their ideas organized, record them talking about the story and what they want to write about.
> 3. Provide them with noise-canceling headphones.
> 4. Allow them to listen to the recording of themselves while writing.

This is a great tactic that I have seen a ton of success with. It allows the student to hear, in their own words, what needs to be written. Remember, ADHD is a disorder of working memory. Holding all of that information in mind during the long, drawn-out, boring writing process is asking a lot of a child. Being able to hear the topics of the story over and over again is like having a mental sticky note constantly given to them while they are writing. Also, this is in their own voice—not a parent, teacher, or other adult, which, as we all know, tends to go in one ear and out the other.

The earlier they get started using this accommodation, the better. If we can allow a child to feel competent and capable in their writing skills at an early age, it sets them up for greater academic success for the rest of their life.

Another effective strategy for writing involves the creation of a "vision board." Most adults think of a vision board as something they create with their friends to help them set lifelong goals, using pictures of extravagant things like a giant mansion, a massive yacht, or a vacation on a tropical island. But vision boards are also an effective tool for students, especially those with ADHD and deficits in NVWM and visual imagery. Allowing children to create visuals based on what they want to write helps with so many of the internal deficits that the ADHD brain needs to overcome.

If the child is able to create even a basic representation of the story in a beginner's comic book format, this would be quite beneficial. Drawing out the end results is an effective form of brainstorming and planning. They can draw the characters, the setting, the conflict, and the resolution all in their own unique and individual way. The best thing about this approach is that there is no right or wrong—all of these things are up to the child's creativity.

If the child is unable to draw, they can get images off the Internet by searching Google Images. They can also use various computer programs to draw and create the images they need. Once all of these images are together in a story format, we will see that the student is more able to get past that ADHD paralysis. As the student starts writing, allow them full access to a dictionary, a thesaurus, and Grammarly so that they have all the tools they need.

Throughout the writing process, one-on-one feedback sessions with the teacher can help students stay on track. The teacher and the student can chunk out pieces of the writing together, and the teacher can fade support over time. Bringing one-on-one attention to this process works very well with the ADHD brain.

Teachers or parents can provide the student with noise-canceling headphones to listen to music without words while they work. Do not allow the student to choose the music themselves—they will just pick their favorite songs and get distracted by them. Offer only classical music or any soothing music that does not have language in it.

We'll also want to allow the student to write in a unique, safe, and comfortable space. Everyone remembers that one teacher they had in middle school or high school who had a couch in their room, or a section of the room with pillows or small tents. These fun little areas allow the child to feel like they are not really at school, like they are somewhere different and cool, where they can be themselves—much like their home living room or basement. This is actually how all GrowNOW clinics are set up—we never want them to look anything like a doctor's office or typical therapist office. We purposely make them look like a student's living room so they can feel comfortable and progress can be more easily transitioned into the natural environment.

I mentioned earlier that a key part of supporting students' literacy skills is addressing how they feel emotionally about reading and writing. Think about it: even for adults, it's a lot easier to self-motivate toward an enjoyable activity than one that feels like a huge chore. There are a number of steps you can take at home and in your child's IEP or 504 to ensure that reading is not something they dread but rather a preferred task.

While the child is reading, set a continuous timer that goes off every five minutes. When the timer goes off, the child should put the book down and explain to you out loud what they just read. This strategy allows them to slowly chunk out the material and not get overwhelmed with having to read too many pages. It also gives them the opportunity to discuss the reading out loud and hear about it in their own words. This provides extra processing time for them to really understand what they are reading and to internalize the information. As the child's reading skills progress, you can extend the timer to go off every 10 minutes, 15 minutes, 20 minutes, and eventually every 30 minutes.

Use the camera app or voice recording app on your phone to record these check-ins during the reading process. When the child is done reading for the day, they can go back and listen to their recordings. They can also listen to the recordings before they start reading again the next day.

One question I often get from parents is "Are audiobooks bad? Are they considered a screen?" Absolutely not. Audiobooks are awesome. They are also an effective strategy for helping students learn to love reading. Have them listen to the audiobook of a story before or after reading it themselves. This can deepen their overall understanding. If a movie adaptation exists, that is also an awesome tool to get the child more engaged!

Many accommodations that work well for writing are just as helpful for reading. Noise-canceling headphones with soothing music and being able to read in a cool, comforting, safe environment, like a couch or "cool-down corner," are always great accommodations. I have also seen a lot of success with students who are able to use visual tools to represent the material they are reading, similar to the vision boards used for writing. They can create their own "webs" of information, either during their regular breaks while reading or when they are finished. This gives them the chance to use their creativity to either draw or use Google Images to show what they are reading about. Reviewing this board each time they read helps the information about the story stick in their working memory. Also, it adds an individual and creative element into reading, strongly increasing the motivation and engagement factor.

Individuals with ADHD often get very caught up in how slow reading is, and they will tell themselves that they do not read fast enough. This causes them to mentally check out and never truly enjoy reading. Allow students to read at whatever speed is comfortable for them without time limits that will make them feel rushed. Ensure that they learn and understand that reading speed is a meaningless statistic. Everyone reads at their own pace, and fast reading is not a requirement for successful reading. Reading should be a creative, comforting, and therapeutic process for them. Not something that makes them feel worse about themselves.

Practice makes perfect. Remember, kids with ADHD should be reading as much as, or even more than, their neurotypical peers. As kids get more comfortable reading independently, books are the ideal replacement for screens, especially at night. Really, this should be a daily requirement. Put the screens away and read in bed. This structure in the home will help kids develop the internal self-motivation to read, and it will also save a lot of nighttime battles for parents.

Study Skills

A common concern for students with ADHD is that they are "poor test takers." When you speak to the parents, they will often say, "I feel like she just doesn't even know *how* to study." This statement is said as if studying is a major skill that needs to be taught. However, let's take a bit of a deeper dive to see why this is such a common problem for students with ADHD.

What do we know about studying? It definitely does not provide any sort of instant gratification. Students may study for a test Thursday evening, take the test Friday, and not get the results until Monday or Tuesday.

There it is again, that one thing that really negatively impacts the ADHD brain—a delay. There is typically always a significant delay between studying and getting the score you've earned as a result of that studying. This causes students with ADHD to have great difficulty building the cause-and-effect relationship in their minds regarding studying intensively and its positive impact on grades. It will take the ADHD student much longer to understand the positives of studying as compared to their neurotypical classmate.

Another truth about studying—it is incredibly boring! Remember, ADHD brains are wired to seek out stimulation through activities that provide bursts of dopamine. And studying is usually just the opposite. To sit and study for a significant amount of time and review the same information over and over requires a massive amount of executive functioning. First, you must have the self-awareness to know that you have a test coming up and to realize that you need to study now so that you are prepared for it. This also requires NVWM and the foresight to look into the future to know the test is coming. And even if you understand logically that you need to study for an upcoming test, you will still need self-motivation to kick-start the process.

Next comes the real difficult part. You are going to have to sustain a very high level of self-regulation and self-motivation over a long period of time to ensure that you are able to study effectively without getting distracted or just giving up in favor of something more stimulating.

NVWM will be needed for hindsight, to gain strength in the moment by remembering a time you studied in the past and it worked out well for you, because you secured a good grade as a result of that hard work.

This is not a "not knowing how to study" issue, this is a self-regulation and self-motivation issue. This is a lack of executive function skills.

To strengthen study skills, we must first strengthen executive functions and the ability to persevere through difficult tasks. It is much easier to strengthen this skill if teachers and parents start working on it while the child is young. It will be far more difficult to convince a middle school student to start studying, when they have been able to successfully avoid the task for this long.

During the later elementary years, around third or fourth grade, teachers should provide direct instruction on different ways to study. This includes re-reading materials, reviewing flash cards, using Quizlet, and getting quizzed by a parent. This introduces their young minds to the various ways to study and, most importantly, teaches them that there is no right or wrong way to do it—it's all about time and effort.

At this age, teachers have a great opportunity to make studying fun and engaging. It's quite easy to do this with programs like Kahoot!, which turns studying into a team-based game show. This is a great task to do at school to bring energy and competition into studying.

When a big test or quiz is coming up, teachers should dedicate blocks of class time to silent independent studying so students can build self-regulation and self-motivation skills toward specific tasks. This should look much like silent reading time, where students have a physical book in hand and are asked to read silently for a period of time, which I am a huge fan of.

During this independent study time, students should have zero access to technology. Any school laptops or tablets should be fully turned off and put away. Because this studying task is so boring and nonstimulating, it is unrealistic to expect students to stay on task and keep reviewing class material while a laptop connected to the Internet, basically a slot machine, is sitting right in front of them. Students should be studying with print books, notes, and worksheets. Teachers may also want to put them in groups of two or a bit larger to help bring the social context in and find ways to make studying fun and competitive.

As students move into middle school and high school, it is still a core recommendation for teachers to allow for study time in class. It is much easier to get the students to put the tech away and stay on the task of studying while they are at school. We are looking to build up their frustration tolerance toward studying by slowly providing opportunities for them to practice in a controlled environment. With scaffolding and fading prompts, we can help them strengthen this self-motivation skill.

At home, with younger kids, studying can be turned into a game with parents and/or siblings. Find a way for them to celebrate their correct answers, maybe by shooting a basketball or jumping onto a giant pile of pillows and blankets. As the parent, you are always modeling persistence (Leonard et al. 2021), especially during this difficult and nonstimulating task of studying.

As children get older and begin their quest for control and independence, they are no longer going to want to study with parents, and that's okay. We will respect that. But that does not mean we let them study independently with their school computers and cell phones in hand. You know nothing productive is happening with those things around, and you're right. Have discussions with the classroom teacher about a physical study packet and what materials need to be printed out so the teen can effectively study. Studying with paper, pen, flash cards, and a set of highlighters will always be far more beneficial than studying with tech (Mueller and Oppenheimer 2014).

There is a very high probability that your child is not able to study within the walls of their home, as it is far too safe, unstructured, and distracting. It's hard to sit and study for a few hours when your parents are close by, and you know how entertaining it would be to get in a nice argument with them. That's a heck of a lot more fun than studying.

Again, parents may want to find a different location for their child to study: at an aunt's, uncle's, or grandparent's house; the local library; or, even better, with a peer. Reach out to parents of other kids in your child's class. There is no doubt there are other moms and dads who are just as stressed about the lack of studying as you are. Find a way for your kids to start a study group together. They can take turns teaching each other the material and quizzing each other. This works just as well with boys and girls, the boys will just complain more. Complaining does not mean cannot. Ignore it. You know what's best for them; they don't.

If your child needs tech to study, there are ways to lock their device on an educational app. All Apple devices have a tool called Guided Access. You may know about Guided Access for nonverbal students who use a device to communicate. When Guided Access is active, the device is locked on the communication app, so the student can't get out of it and start playing games. It becomes a dedicated communication device and can be used for nothing else. You are able to use this tool to make your child's tablet a dedicated educational device, not one for entertainment and distraction.

Test it on your own phone first. Go into Settings on your Apple phone or tablet and search for "Guided Access."

You will set a secret password, which you obviously do not share with your child, to lock the device on Google Classroom or whatever app they need to study. They will no longer be able to leave Google Classroom and start watching YouTube videos of other people playing video games. Google "Guided Access" to learn more about how it works. Guardrails like these give kids a real opportunity to acquire the internal self-motivation they'll need to be successful students.

Self-Improvement

One of my main priorities over the past few years has been doing intake calls with parents who are interested in learning more about GrowNOW services. And one of the most common things I hear on those intake calls is "My child is never going to agree to do coaching! He doesn't even think he has a problem! He just thinks we are so annoying and always on his back."

Every parent explains as if only their child is like this. If there's one thing about special needs parenting, it's the feeling of isolation. The feeling that nobody gets it, nobody understands what you go through, nobody can ever comprehend the internal struggle you deal with every day. But, of course, these parents are far from alone.

The truth is that of the thousands of ADHD students we have ever worked with at GrowNOW, the vast majority, probably about 99%, were seriously against having to do coaching sessions when their parents first brought it up to them. This greatly concerns the parents, as parents today really struggle with hearing their child complain, be uncomfortable, and have to do things they don't want to do. They are, of course, also concerned that they will spend money on the sessions and the child will just hate it the entire time and barely participate.

But what parents need to understand is that this is ADHD in a nutshell. First, it is a disorder of self-awareness, so kids with ADHD will typically not realize that there's a problem at all. It is hard for them to fully understand how different they may be from their peers. And ADHD is a disorder of self-motivation so they do not want to do anything new or outside of their comfort zone. This is a basic fact of parenting a child with ADHD: you cannot wait for them to want to make changes or grow their skills. They do not have the self-motivation to do this. You need to help them develop that self-motivation.

Parents are often stuck in this mindset that they need to convince their kids to do something new. But this is false. When it comes to things that are necessary for your child's long-term success, you do not need to get their full buy-in immediately. You have to get comfortable stepping into your parental authority and asking your kids to do things they'd rather not. At some point, we all need to learn this major life skill: doing things you don't want to do at first and, later, learning to love it. I talked earlier about how, if your school offers the option, you need to sign your child up for homework club, no matter how they feel about it. That's a perfect example.

Because school is one of the core areas where children with ADHD will struggle with self-motivation, there are several methods teachers will want to use to increase engagement and buy-in. For students with ADHD, one of the simplest and most effective teaching strategies is to develop a relationship with the student. Teachers need to be able to be themselves and share their fun personalities. Students love when their teachers do this—when they deviate from the norm, stop talking about the basic academics, and show their students their fun side.

Go ahead and think about some of your favorite teachers you had as a child. The ones who left a lasting impression on you to this day. Was it the teacher who was just so amazing at giving lectures and made it easy to learn? Or was it the teacher who often took breaks from teaching to share stories about their personal lives, tell jokes, and discuss materials away from the curriculum? People respond positively to relationships, rapport, and warmth. This is especially true for children. When teachers are able to be their true selves and have some fun, students naturally feel safe and engaged in the classroom.

The only way to create this warmth is for teachers to have real conversations with students, just as they would have with their friends outside of school (minus the cursing and adult language). These conversations cannot be about grades, schoolwork, homework, or any academic subject.

Meet with ADHD students one on one to talk about preferred interests. School may not be their preferred task, but other things definitely are. It is up to the teacher to find out what makes this child tick, such as what gets this child energized and motivated and what their absolute favorite things are to do in their free and unstructured time. Ideally, at home, parents are following the obvious research and have eliminated screens, but if they haven't, there's a good chance that this child's preferred interests involve video games, YouTube videos, and memes. Discussing these things with the child can really make a difference, even if it is incredibly annoying for the teacher to do. If you know absolutely nothing about their preferred interest, have them teach you. Kids love to take on the "teacher role" and educate others about things they love. These interactions allow teachers to form authentic bonds with their students, and that will go a long way in helping kids find the self-motivation to actively participate in their education.

PART IV

Self-Evaluation

## PART IV

Self-Protection

CHAPTER 10

The Final Pillar

Developing True Independence

Meet Mia, a 12-year-old girl. Like many kids with ADHD, Mia often interrupts conversations, dominates social interactions with her ideas, and acts impulsively without considering how her friends feel. And, as another result of her ADHD, she struggles with self-evaluation.

One afternoon, Mia invites her best friend, Emily, to hang out. They start watching a movie, but after a few minutes, Mia gets bored and wants to play a game instead. Emily is still interested in the movie and asks to keep watching. Rather than compromising, Mia ignores Emily's input and starts to set up the game. Emily is a little upset but tries to go along with the new plan.

A few minutes later, Mia becomes frustrated when Emily accidentally knocks over some game pieces. In a burst of impulsive anger, Mia yells, "You ruined it!" and storms out of the room. Emily, feeling hurt and embarrassed, decides to leave early. The next day at school, Emily doesn't sit with Mia during lunch, and over the next few weeks, they start spending less time together.

Mia is aware that Emily has started avoiding her, but she doesn't know why. Without being able to understand what went wrong, she winds up making the same mistakes in her other relationships. Despite gentle reminders from her parents and teachers to "stop and think," Mia can't seem to keep from repeating these same missteps—interrupting, not compromising, acting impulsively—over and over again. She feels like she's constantly losing friends, but she's unable to see that her own behavior is the cause.

As these social struggles pile up, Mia's self-image begins to suffer. She starts to feel like she's bad at making friends or that other kids just don't like her. Because she can't evaluate her own behavior effectively, she internalizes this social rejection as a personal flaw rather than a pattern of actions she can change.

Mia's inability to learn from past mistakes and adjust her behavior fuels a negative cycle: the more she struggles with social interactions, the more her confidence drops. Her low self-esteem makes her more likely to withdraw from social situations out of fear of rejection. Her isolation is perpetuated, and the cycle continues.

Stuck in the Time Loop

It's like Groundhog Day. Every day, the same fights, the same arguments, the same mistakes made over and over. Your child simply is not building the connections between studying and getting improved grades, sharing with others and building friendships, keeping their hands to themselves and not losing their preferred tasks or items. No matter what you do, you feel they never learn.

Parenting an ADHD child means dealing with the same issues time and time again, and that's a major reason why so many of these parents end up divorced or needing therapy themselves.

Every single day, parents of kids with ADHD will get a call that has become familiar: their child's teacher reporting how their child misbehaved or acted out at school.

"Tommy called out 10 times and was highly disruptive to the rest of the class. I was not able to get through my lesson."

"Veronica continued to threaten Mary with being kicked out of the group chat with all of their friends."

"Bailey broke every rule in gym class today and we were never able to begin our structured soccer game."

Most teachers, who are no doubt overworked and underpaid all across the country, do not get formal training on ADHD and executive functioning during their bachelor's level program. They are also in charge of the education and safety of anywhere from 10 to 100 children per day. There is no way they have the time to effectively deal with these actions as they come up. All they can do is call the parent and inform them of what happened.

But what is the parent going to do? By the time the child gets home, these actions and behaviors are completely out of their mind. This puts the family members in a difficult position. As the parent of an ADHD child, you've probably heard a lot about how your kid needs to experience "natural consequences," but maybe you've been there, done that—and they are left completely unbothered.

When your ADHD child hits their sibling, you might raise your voice a bit and explain how "we do not hit in this family" while keeping the crying sibling in front of them so they can understand what they did. You may try to reason over and over again with your child about what they can earn if they finish their homework. But none of it makes any difference. No change in their behavior, choices, or impulsive acts, no matter the consequence, no matter the reward.

When things go wrong, these kids rarely take time to think about why it all went so poorly or how it could have gone better. Their brains don't have a built-in mechanism for self-reflection. Instead, as soon as an event is over, they move on without considering how to avoid or recreate similar situations in the future. They are constantly onto the next thing. As a result, it is extremely difficult for them to pause and reflect on their actions and then make changes accordingly.

As parents or teachers, it's tempting to offer suggestions and corrections. But usually, that just doesn't do any good. Even when adults or peers point out where a kid with ADHD has misstepped, they frequently have trouble internalizing the feedback. They might feel overwhelmed or react defensively rather than making meaningful changes to their behavior. The inability to make different, better decisions leads to one mistake after another after another.

This is all part of the executive functioning skill of self-evaluation: the ability to not just remember past events but look at them critically, learn from them, and apply those lessons to the present. Strong self-evaluation skills are our best defense against repeating mistakes or negative acts.

People with strong self-evaluative abilities are able to recall their past experiences and use those memories to make healthier and happier choices in the present moment—to truly be more educated. This is exactly what life is all about: to grow and learn each day, month, and year of our lives and to experience as much as we possibly can so we know about the world and its people.

One essential component of self-evaluation, like all other executive functions, is nonverbal working memory and, specifically, hindsight. Individuals with ADHD will often have greatly diminished self-evaluation skills, due in large part to their impaired NVWM.

I have worked with students who, when asked to use their NVWM, can literally only see themselves in a small white room, with nothing around them. No details, no movement, no actions. Many of them start with a NVWM system that I refer to as fifties black-and-white grainy television. This is not good, and this skill needs practice immediately.

Without developing NVWM and self-evaluation skills, ADHD individuals forge through life in ways that few others can truly understand. We want to be able to learn from our mistakes, fit in, be successful, and not be at the constant mercy of our impulses. As adults, we will often try to rehearse an experience in our mind, maybe while we are in the car alone on the way to a social event. We will mentally practice over and over not to bring up that same terrible joke, not to make that offensive comment, but to be an active listener instead of talking over people, to ask people questions about themselves to see how they're doing, and to actually listen to their answers! But even these mental rehearsals don't always help.

The ability to truly self-evaluate, learn from the past, remember how we made ourselves and others feel, and apply that to our present behaviors is so much more difficult than anyone can put into words. This is what leads to ADHD burnout and so much isolation and negative self-talk: "Why even keep trying to make friends, when all I do is fail every single time? I'm tired of being the one who gets roasted and made fun of every time we all get together. I am better off just going home and scrolling through my phone for hours."

You can see the problem here. Social difficulties will often drive kids deeper into digital dependency or addiction, which makes it even harder to gain the skills they're missing. The more they use screens, the more they miss out on chances for both social growth and executive function development. Increased digital media use is directly linked with poor communication skills, a lack of empathy, and a weakened ability to interpret emotions (Muppalla et al. 2023), and that, of course, leads to yet more social rejection and isolation. Ultimately, kids may face feelings of loneliness and total dependency on digital interactions.

Beyond its impact on social skills, self-evaluation is also critical for setting goals and making personal and academic progress. Recognizing our success or failure in areas that are important to us is a key part of self-evaluation. But the digital world's constant rewards can cause kids to become detached from their real-life goals, less able to reflect on progress, and less capable of assessing their performance. And as we've already discussed, the motivation and reward systems of developing brains are profoundly impacted by excessive screen use (George et al. 2023).

As kids move into adult life, self-evaluation becomes more important than ever. If we allow screens to impair this ability, we're setting them up for a lifetime of avoidable challenges. Screens negatively influence the development of analytical skills needed to solve complex problems, plan effectively, and make sound decisions—all of which are necessary for academic as well as professional and personal success. Screen-induced effects like impulsivity, difficulty delaying gratification, and poor emotional regulation can all contribute to financial mismanagement later in life. With stunted executive functions, poor work habits, and cognitive delays (Presta et al. 2024), screen-dependent kids are less likely to be able to secure stable jobs when they grow up. Not to mention that even before screens, people with ADHD have, on average, significantly lower lifetime earnings than neurotypical people.

Whether you're looking at social relationships, financial security, emotional well-being, or any other aspect of life success—there is so much at stake here.

Unlocking a Better Future

The constant stimulation, the incessant instant gratification, and the extinction of play and boredom are hurting our children and perpetuating the worst youth mental health crisis in history. But, with patience and diligence, we can fight back.

Let's be honest, all of us in life want a "quick fix" to our problems. There is a reason why parents ask me on intake calls, "How long until we're going to see progress?" They ask me this before I ever even meet their child. This is obviously a highly unethical question to answer because every single child is so different. But I get it. We want our problems to go away as quickly and as inexpensively as possible. Parents want their kids to be independent and compliant, and teachers want their students to stay on task, take notes, get good grades, not call out, stay organized, and follow all directions—all overnight. This is not a fault. This is human nature.

One of the main things we express to parents when they sign their kids up for coaching, and to teachers when they first start to implement our strategies, is this: progress will not happen overnight. All good things take time.

There are ways to improve self-evaluation. It's not quick, and it's usually not easy. But it can be done.

The goal for our kids is to bring their NVWM system from that grainy black-and-white TV to 2025 HDTV, with all the details, colors, and features. Once we get to this point, kids will have a much better ability to visualize the past as well as the future, which is a crucial building block of effective self-evaluation.

When we equip children with the tools to think about their past experiences and memories, to visualize and imagine the future through predictions, and to evaluate themselves and their actions, we are strengthening the foundation of the greatest skill set for human beings: executive functions. When we help children feel emotionally engaged in their own success by no longer just focusing on the present moment, and instead bringing the past and future into the equation, we see incredible results.

CHAPTER 11

The Playbook on Self-Evaluation

Self-evaluation skills are required to make the improvements we need to grow through life. We have to learn from our past to make tomorrow better than yesterday. If we keep repeating our yesterdays, we go nowhere, and we are simply not prepared for our futures.

Self-evaluation combines our other pillars—self-awareness, self-regulation, self-motivation—and adds the ability to introspect and the desire to improve and grow. The development of self-evaluation is what allows children to move beyond their comfort zone, learn from their mistakes, and successfully transition into an independent adulthood.

Moving Beyond the Comfort Zone

Executive functions come from experiences—varied experiences. Every single day looks different from the last, and that allows us to gain new insights and new skills. But this is not what the ADHD brain wants. The ADHD brain wants the comfort zone. They want every day to look the same while they are in complete control. When there is no discomfort, no challenge, and no delayed gratification, there's no need for self-regulation, self-motivation, or self-evaluation.

To make matters worse, screens have redefined what "control" looks and feels like. The ability to control something with your fingers, endless entertainment in the form of videos, memes, notifications, upgrades, likes, shares—it's just too much. ADHD brains cannot handle all of this.

Because of the screen epidemic, many kids today experience life as one big nonpreferred task after another: school, homework, chores and roles in the house, basic hygienic tasks, and even face-to-face socialization. The proportion of time children spend in the comfort zone on only preferred tasks is getting larger, while time spent outside of it continues to dwindle. Less time outside the comfort zone means less time to develop life-altering executive function skills.

One of the most important things for parents to accept is that your child with ADHD does not know what is best for them. They will need you, the strong, authoritative parent, to push them into nonpreferred, new, challenging tasks every single day to get them out of their small and narrow ADHD comfort zone.

You are the parent; you are the adult. You have the ability to see into the future. You understand cause and effect. You can see how doing a specific healthy and positive task now, such as joining the chess club or art club, can benefit them and their future. With their ADHD, they cannot see this themselves. They will need you to do their evaluation for them. The problem is, they won't like it in the moment.

I am here to tell you exactly what you know but are too afraid to admit. It is something you've been thinking for a very long time but never had the courage to utter: if you have an ADHD child, you cannot have screens in your house.

Parents—you know screens are a problem. A huge problem. You know it's hurting them and their development and relationships. You know the overuse is dysregulating them.

You know your only option is to remove the screens.

I have worked with more than 500 families who successfully eliminated screens. When I first told them that screens had to go, they all had the same face. Absolutely frozen in fear. Blankly staring at me, stone cold. So unbelievably scared. How could they not be? This is a difficult thing to do and to endure.

When I have this discussion with parents, it's actually quite fascinating how they instantly go into "survival mode" to figure out how to make this easier on them. They begin to ask many questions to look for ways to make it as little of a fight as possible.

What we have to do is stop and take a bird's-eye view of this. If I was a parent coach and I told you that you needed to remove your child's LEGOs, action figures, books, magazines, etc.—you would think, "Okay, cool. No problem! I will go do that right now." But when it's screens, parents are terrified of what might happen. That right there is all the proof you need of exactly why you have to do it! This isn't some toy we're talking about; this is a drug.

You are not scared of their dysregulated behaviors—you are already dealing with that every single day. This is something totally different and much more frightening to parents. These are withdrawals. Your child is withdrawing from a drug they are addicted to, and they will do whatever they possibly can to get it back. They will use every tool they have—anger, whining, complaining, followed by physical aggression, property destruction, yelling, provoking sympathy, threatening—everything they possibly can to control this situation. Because this is what screens have taught their brains: that they can be in full control all the time. This is what is so addicting about it. So they will do whatever they can to get that drug back, especially when it comes to the parents who took them away and can return them. Their addiction tells them, "I can get my screens back if I make things as uncomfortable for my parents as possible."

I have worked with numerous families who have actually had to call 911 to ensure everyone's safety. Calling 911 on your child is not easy. But that is how serious this addiction is. Whether it is self-harm, threats of self-harm, property destruction, physically attacking others, or massive panic attacks—this is the stronghold that screens have on our children's brains.

When you are a family that has to remove screens from your child, safety is, and always will be, the highest priority. You will need to do everything in your power to ensure your child and family are safe. If that means you need to call emergency services, do not hesitate to do so. Sometimes, the addiction is so extreme, professional help is needed. Parents cannot do everything themselves—even though they often try to.

One thing I want all parents to remember: it is not your fault if your child is addicted to screens, especially if they have ADHD. You gave your child screens with the best of intentions as they were pushed into your life relentlessly by both advertising and social pressures. I'm sure your child also nagged you a bit to get the phone and games. But it is your responsibility to remove them if you see it is a problem or it is stunting their development. It's one of the hardest things you'll do, but you know it's necessary.

Sometimes a child's withdrawal behaviors last for two to four weeks. It takes the child time to realize that none of their tactics or behaviors is going to work. It takes time for their brain to detox. Parents have to stay strong and keep those screens away permanently. They have to persevere through every single behavior their kid uses and stay focused on their long-term goals for their child. They have to remind themselves that this is all temporary, and there is light at the end of the tunnel.

When you take this on, ensure you have a support system. Have aunts, uncles, grandparents, neighbors, coaches, counselors, and peers who can also hold your child accountable. You can't do this all on your own!

If we want kids to have a successful life, we need them to have a real childhood. A childhood is filled with time spent with peers and daily outdoor play, even in high school. Parents, the power to provide this kind of childhood is in your hands.

Screens may make them happy now, in the moment. But they are sure to dysregulate them later. And they are sure to hold them back from what they need for the future. Screens are hurting and significantly delaying your child's executive function skills.

As parents, are you parenting for today, or for the day when you can no longer be their parent?

Don't let screens steal your child from outdoor play.

Don't let screens steal your child from varied experiences.

Don't let screens steal your child from real relationships.

Don't let screens steal your child from independence.

Don't let screens steal your child from the greatest predictor of success: executive function skills.

The more time your child spends out of the house, away from parents and screens, around other adults and peers, the better for their development. There is never any growth within the comfort zone.

Learning from the Past

The mistake your child made yesterday that led to yelling, crying, and broken property? It's going to happen again today and will happen tomorrow.

Because of their delayed self-evaluation, children with ADHD exhibit little to no ability to learn from past experiences and apply them to the present so they do not repeat the same mistakes over and over. They also exhibit little ability to forecast themselves in the future so they can effectively plan, prioritize, problem solve, and delay gratification.

This brings us to my predictions and review model. I designed this model by following the research and working closely with hundreds of education professionals. Teachers continually expressed to me that the expensive "curriculums" they'd purchased and trained in-depth on did absolutely nothing to move the needle. Worksheets and manuals hadn't helped at all. They were left still not understanding executive functioning at school. What they needed were strategies that were simple and quick, so they still had enough time to teach their main curriculum. They needed a basic set of principles that would get all of their students engaged and ready to learn.

To do this, we had to bring NVWM and VWM into the classroom, each and every day. After years of work, we had the predictions and review model—and the progress and success started pouring in.

The predictions and review model follows these steps.

First, class will begin with the teacher asking students to put their heads down and close their eyes. The teacher then provides this prompt: "Let's all make a mental movie of how we predict this class will go today! What do you think we will talk about? What do you think we will do? How will it all make you feel? What are some things you expect to happen, and what might surprise you?" Then, the teacher starts a one-minute timer.

This is an important first step—and as with all executive functioning, it starts with NVWM. We are providing the students a natural and organic way to build this skill.

This is a skill that rarely gets to be practiced these days in this world of screens and instant gratification. Head down, eyes closed, left with nothing but their own imagination.

This is purposefully done for many reasons. First, the students will have to call on the hindsight of their NVWM to remember what they did in class yesterday. This is so simple, yet so powerful. How often are today's students just going through the motions and not connecting the dots between days and lessons? This allows them to think deeply about what the content was yesterday and automatically become more engaged in what's going on, because they want to get this right. They want to remember accurately.

Then, based on their NVWM's hindsight, the students will use the foresight in their NVWM and their imagination to make inferences and predictions about what might happen today. Over time, this becomes very fun for the students. They like to make guesses about things that are flexible, where the stakes are not as high as a right-or-wrong test question. They are able to think about what might happen in class today and, most importantly, how they might feel about it. Will it make them feel positive and engaged, or do they already expect to get bored and distracted or feel inadequate?

The timer will go off, prompting students to pick up their heads and re-enter the classroom community. The teacher will then ask the class, "Please raise your hand and share some of your predictions." If nobody raises their hand, the teacher will call on select students. They will ask specific questions to elicit information about the students' mental movies:

- What did that feel like?
- Did you have everything with you or did you need any materials?

- Was that interesting or frustrating?
- Did you need help?
- Was anything surprising or different than expected?

One thing we see from the exercise is that it takes a lot of time and practice for students to be able to describe their mental movies in an effective way. There is so much deep comprehension and language processing needed to be able to put their thoughts into words. With time and consistency with this routine, that is one of the main areas of progress we see emerge from this exercise: a greater ability to understand their thoughts and better express themselves. This is foundational for all success in school—comfort and confidence with self-expression.

So far with this model, we have discussed the facets of NVWM. Now, we bring VWM into the equation.

The teacher will decide the best examples of predictions shared by students. They will record these responses on the side of the chalkboard, on a shared Google Doc, etc.—so they can be referred to later.

The teacher then provides this prompt: "Based on what you saw in your mental movies, what are some things you can say to your brain coach when these things happen? If you start to feel bored or get distracted, what can you say to your brain to get back on task?" The students' responses might sound like this:

- "If (student name) calls out in the middle of class, then we can tell our brain not to respond and stay focused."
- "If I feel like I am getting lost and falling behind, then I can ask my brain how to phrase the question, and then I will raise my hand and have the courage to ask it out loud."

- "If we are going to work in teams, then I am going to speak and contribute, instead of being passive and sitting back. I am going to be a strong and valuable team member."
- "If I feel tempted, then I am going to talk to my brain and make sure that I do not use my school computer inappropriately. I will not access non-school websites. If I stay focused on the class, then I can perform well on the upcoming test."
- "If another classmate does something unexpected, then I will focus on myself and what I can control—only myself. I will talk to my brain to ensure I stay my best self."

Notice how each of these responses is structured in "if-then" language. We want to encourage this for several reasons. First, we are making predictions, not stating facts—so we want to use the word "if" because nothing is definite. Second, the ADHD brain has a very hard time understanding if-then cause-and-effect thinking. This is due to their lack of NVWM and conditional thinking. It is hard for them to connect the dots between actions and choices and their consequences. This provides an opportunity for them to practice.

The teacher then does what they do best—teach! They follow the lesson plan they created and teach their curriculum, just as they had planned. As I referred to earlier, the best strategies are the ones that do not take a lot of time and still allow teachers to teach and do their jobs. This step takes up the vast majority of the class period.

At the end of class, the teacher brings back the prediction statements they recorded. They read them aloud for the entire class to hear. There is then a quick and powerful discussion about predictions versus reality.

- What turned out better than expected?
- What was an unexpected struggle?
- How did we end up feeling about how this class went?
- Did we perform as our best selves?
- Did we stay engaged with our brain coach?
- What was something that you found interesting/boring?
- Did you accomplish your goals?
- How can we be even better tomorrow?

When I train schools on the most up-to-date research on executive functioning, many of them opt in for a long-term consulting relationship. In these relationships, my absolute favorite thing to see is how, over time, the students' predictions start to become more and more aligned with reality. The growth that students show when teachers stay consistent with this program is a beautiful thing to witness.

There are many schools I have consulted with and classrooms I have observed from the start of the year in late August or early September. In the month of September, many of the students will not take this task seriously, and they'll make silly jokes about their predictions. This is normal, and it is completely okay! We as adults do this too when we are tasked with something new and out of the ordinary. When we start a new job and are faced with the discomfort of a steep learning curve, we make little jokes to alleviate the stress. The same happens when we meet new people, start a new sport, or head back to the gym after a long hiatus.

For the teachers who stay strong and consistent, that silliness goes away. Right around October is when we see the students start to really take this task seriously. They are used to it and have come to expect it, as it is now a daily routine in the classroom. Students are now incredibly eager to put their heads down, make their mental movies, and then share their predictions to see if they come true.

With great consistency, around Halloween and early November, we see the magic happen. We see the dots start to get connected. These students have had enough consistent practice with making mental movies that their NVWM is really beginning to improve. Their mental movies are becoming more vivid and detailed. Now, the students' predictions are becoming aligned with reality.

This sounds so simple, but it is so incredibly profound. We are making these young students future thinkers. We are teaching them through a fun and engaging exercise that it is beneficial to think about and visualize the future. The look on their face when they learn they made a successful prediction is one of my favorite things to see in my career. They made a prediction; it came true. They successfully thought about and predicted the future. This is almost a greater feeling than getting an A+ on a test.

Students are also observed to more effectively deal with obstacles, challenges, and distractions. Because they have become stronger future thinkers, they are now better equipped to handle these stressors as they come. For example, when a student calls out and tries to get stimulated by the laughter of their classmates, the other students learn to completely ignore them, and the behaviors dissipate. Also, we start to see students self-advocate more when they get lost or feel behind in the lecture because they are engaged in more positive and motivating self-talk with their VWM.

Best of all, we start to see students more effectively manage their attention and focus. Distractibility and off-task behavior greatly decreases, because it is no longer "spur of the moment"—the student already thought about their task, visualized it, and prepared for it. They already processed the if-then, cause-and-effect thinking. If I get distracted and go on nonschool websites, I will fall behind and not do well on the test, and I don't like the way that feels. So I will stay on task, do my best, and ensure that I am being my best self at all times.

This is the organic and natural executive function practice that students in today's world need so badly. Not only are these students more emotionally engaged, they feel more comfortable, safe, and confident at a place where they previously felt anxious, uncomfortable, and inadequate: school. When school becomes a place of comfort and confidence, the sky is the limit—not just for the students themselves but also for the teachers.

"Failure to Launch" into Adulthood

The word "accommodation" often has a positive connotation to it, and for good reason. We are accommodating a disability by supporting that person and their needs. Much of this is all part of the Americans with Disabilities Act, which does amazing things like ensuring buildings have ramps, elevators, and handicap parking spots close to the entrance. It also requires public entities to provide an American Sign Language (ASL) interpreter for those who are deaf or hard of hearing.

Accommodations for children with ADHD should have a single purpose: help the student overcome their executive functioning delay, not "make the student's life easier" or "make the student happy." These students' accommodations should be designed so that eventually they are no longer needed.

When it comes to developing the crucial skills they will need for their lives, such as getting places on time, treating others with kindness and respect, and completing basic tasks, teachers and parents need to have a zero tolerance policy. There are no accommodations in life for those basic things in our society. Your workplace will not allow you to come in late, say rude things to co-workers, and not complete tasks you are getting paid to complete because you have a medical diagnosis and a completed evaluation for ADHD.

One of the most important things you learned by reading this book is the value of the foundational skills of executive function: nonverbal and verbal working memory. Without the foundational skills, there is no learning and no skill acquisition, and school will be one big insurmountable challenge that creates a lot of stress and anxiety.

This is exactly what our current model of education gets so insanely wrong: memorization over understanding, all academics and testing, no executive function. This is one of the many reasons why kids with ADHD get sent to inappropriate therapies, where parents spend thousands but see little progress. It is also why the current IEP and 504 system does not equip students with real-world skills and many are left floundering once they age out.

We are seeing this now with ADHD students who too often become the classic "failure to launch." They reach the age of 18, and that thick IEP and 504 are now gone. Parents are no longer around to constantly do things for them and accommodate them to get through life's daily struggles. It is now on the ADHD teen to learn from their experiences and make healthy, positive choices.

If they cannot self-evaluate, this likely will not happen. They will be stuck in their comfort zone. It won't matter what that IEP or 504 did. If we don't know our past, understand it, and fully internalize it, we are destined to repeat it.

Schools play a part in this, but so do parents. After the child becomes fully capable of doing things on their own, the parents continue doing things for them to avoid fights.

If this codependency and prompt dependency lasts too long, up until senior year of high school, then we are really in a difficult situation. This child is still fully dependent on their parents, and college or work is now on the horizon, and they are nowhere near ready for either.

When it comes to ADHD and executive functioning for children and teens, whose brains are still developing each and every day, we have to be sure we are not over-accommodating them to the point where it is inhibiting internal skill development.

There are plenty of classroom accommodations that can be used to increase accountability and encourage improvements in executive function. For example, accommodations might focus on immediate feedback and reflection. Teachers can provide daily or weekly progress monitoring sheets for the student to self-evaluate their performance in class. Weekly check-ins with a counselor or specialist can help the student review their progress and troubleshoot challenges.

For behavior reinforcement, teachers can establish a tiered system for rewards. They might allow the student to earn points for completed work, which they can redeem for privileges. This helps students become more aware of their behavior and encourages them to track their success. Visual timers or verbal prompts can be an effective aid for increasing the student's sense of urgency and task initiation. An excellent strategy is to assign a peer mentor or buddy for the student to work with, encouraging both students to keep each other accountable. This comes back to the idea of having a peer model to encourage on-task behavior.

An often overlooked idea in IEPs and 504s is increased consequences. Consequences should be clearly defined and immediate. They should also have a logical connection with the offense. Teachers can implement low-stakes consequences, such as the loss of a privilege, paired with opportunities for correction, like completing unfinished work during a study hall.

When inappropriate behavior occurs, students should be required to fill out a behavior reflection form. The form should ask the student what happened, what the result was, and how to address the effects of their actions. And, importantly, the student should be required to follow through on the action they've identified. For example, as part of the accountability process, they might owe someone an apology or otherwise need to make amends.

Classroom accommodations are incredibly useful tools, but we can't forget the single most important teacher kids will have in their lives: their parents. When we talk about preparing kids for adulthood, their parents are the ones modeling what it means to be an adult each and every day.

So many parents out there feel unseen and alone. Every day, they put others before themselves. The cooking, cleaning, organizing, planning—does anyone even notice? Does anyone even care? Your child with ADHD notices. They will probably never come right out and say it, but they see all you do for them and the entire family. This is how they learn—by seeing you be a calm, strong, composed leader. By showing self-motivation and modeling persistence when things get tough. Improving your own executive function skills can be a powerful way to help your children improve theirs.

This is why parent training is one of the core recommendations from the American Academy of Pediatrics (Wolraich et al. 2019). When parents educate themselves and use evidence-based strategies instead of going off their instincts, we see positive growth and change.

CHAPTER 12

ADHD Hope

Writing this book was an emotional and terrifying process for me. It's hard for me to open up, be vulnerable, and talk about myself and my journey. I poured my heart and soul into writing this, all while knowing that people are going to read it and still be left with more questions than answers.

This is obviously a book meant for a large audience—so in no way is it tailored toward unique individuals or unique families. I am sure there were many times you read a suggestion or recommendation and thought "There is no way this is going to work with my kid"—and you might be fully correct on that. This is why individualized parent coaching is so important for ADHD and executive functions—because there is no "one size fits all." Use this book as a starting point, a true playbook to guide you and your family into success and independence—where you can use an unlimited number of audibles—because you know your child best.

The core reason I wrote this book is because I've made it my life's mission to focus on one thing I want to help others with: quality of life.

Because when it comes to ADHD, it's all about quality of life. ADHD is a disorder of the executive functioning system, and executive functions are the greatest predictor of life success. You want to make friends and keep them? You want to get a job and keep that job and income? You want to move out of your parents' house and live independently? You need executive functions. There is no set of skills more crucial to lifelong success, positivity, safety, and health. The more I spread the good word about executive functions, the more people I help. All I want to do is move forward and devote my life toward this mission.

And it's clear that this work is needed. You can make a strong argument that there has never been a more difficult time in history to be a parent. Schools are getting more rigorous, and the implementation of personal laptops for each student has only made things far worse. Students are receiving more homework, and it is all digital, on their laptops, giving parents one more thing to monitor and supervise.

When you are a parent to a child with ADHD, you will inevitably find yourself wearing too many hats. You are no longer just the parent; you are now the executive functioning system for the entire family. You are the homework secretary, the morning chauffeur, the evening drill sergeant, the playdate creator, the schedule keeper.

Every parent of ADHD kids has to take a step back, fully realize what's happening, and say to themselves, "I am doing too much." Start to look at each individual area where you are doing too much: "In the morning routine, I am playing a cat-and-mouse game every single morning. There isn't a single day that we are not rushing out the door behind schedule, causing them to be late for school, and causing me to be late for work. Every single day there is a fight over homework. Every night, the bedtime routine is a disaster, and nobody gets to bed on time."

We have to accept that we are doing too much, and the "doing too much" strategy just isn't working.

As a parent, you are doing everything with the best of intentions. You love your child unconditionally, and it is so hard to watch them be late, fail, and not live up to the expectations you may have envisioned for them. You know your child depends on you for every little thing. Without you, their life would be pure chaos. Deep in your heart, the hardest possible thing is to even think about doing less.

But this is not a system that works, and this is not a system that lasts. Your child needs you to step back. Your child needs you to do less. They cannot develop independent skills without experiencing life on their own—the good and the bad.

Do we want them to develop executive function skills, gain independence, and be successful on their own? If we truly want that, we have to look at ourselves first before we look at them. If parents do too much and inject themselves into every aspect of their child's life, the child will not develop these skills, and this vicious cycle will continue for years. This is by far the hardest part of ADHD parenting—learning how to fade back, do less, and allow your child to experience life.

Final Note on Screens

Overindulge your child to avoid conflict.

This is the simplest definition of permissive parenting. This is where parents of children with ADHD often find themselves when they have screens in the house.

Even for neurotypical children, overuse of screens is associated with:

- ♦ Decreased executive functioning (Liu et al. 2022)
- ♦ Inattentiveness (McArthur et al. 2020)

- Dysregulation (Presta et al. 2024)
- Lower cognitive abilities (Presta et al. 2024)
- Lower academic performance (Liu et al. 2022; George et al. 2023)
- Decreased language skills (McArthur et al. 2020)
- Aggressive behavior (McArthur et al. 2020; George et al. 2023)
- Decreased social skills (McArthur et al. 2020; George et al. 2023)
- Sleep disturbances (Liu et al. 2022; George et al. 2023)
- Depression (George et al. 2023)

For that list I just provided, you can remove the term "overuse of screens" and replace it with "symptoms of ADHD." Is this why ADHD diagnosis rates have skyrocketed over the past five years, to the point where we now have Adderall shortages? I am not entirely sure, but it is a question we must ask. At the same time, we have also vastly improved our awareness around it, so it's possible that it's being detected more easily. One thing we are sure of is that screens do not cause ADHD. ADHD is a congenital brain difference, most often caused by one or both parents having it themselves (Grimm et al. 2020).

Screens have created an uphill battle for parents they feel they simply cannot win. One simple piece of advice I tell parents—the behaviors you are seeing are communication. Your kids are communicating with you and sending you a message via their dysregulation. What they are most often saying to you with these behaviors is "My brain is not ready for this. I cannot handle this level of stimulation yet." Here are some more basic red flags to look out for:

- Does your child constantly ask for a screen?
- Do you already limit their access to screens, but they are still constantly dysregulated?

- Do you constantly find yourself offering or threatening to take away screen time to get your child to do every basic task? For example: "If you don't brush your teeth now, you will lose screen time all day tomorrow!" or "If you finish your homework, you will earn 30 extra minutes of screen time!"

If any of these three red flags are present in your home, the most important thing for you to do is to ensure that your house is screen-free.

No video games. No computer games. No tablets.

Let's face the truth—in today's world of insanely addictive screens, this everlasting dream of a "balance" does not work anymore, and it is just not realistic. There's a reason why children cannot drink alcohol, vote, or drive. They simply cannot have all these screens for the same reason: their brains are not ready. I have never met a child with ADHD who did not get dysregulated in some way by screens.

Even schools are giving them screens now. Edtech has thrown a massive wrench into American education and the daily lives of the American family. Do edtech companies realize this or even care? Or is it just about the dollar signs?

A colleague of mine, Emily Cherkin, known as TheScreentimeConsultant on Instagram, specializes in exposing the truth about edtech. She posted that in 2013 Bill Gates was quoted as saying, "We won't know for a decade if edtech will work." Well, 10 years later, a UNESCO (2023) report showed that more screen time means lower well-being. Since edtech invaded our schools, billions were spent (edtech Evidence Exchange 2021), test scores declined (Mumphrey 2023), and mental health worsened (Olfson et al. 2015; National Center for Health Statistics 2023). The answer to Bill Gates' question was loud and clear: edtech has been a colossal failure.

The number of parents I hear from today who say they can't take screens away because their child is a competitive gamer or wants to be a YouTuber never ceases to amaze me, not only because of the insanely small percentage of kids for whom this will actually become a lifelong career but also that parents are allowing them to do these things all day every day when they have a childhood to experience. Sure, you want to be a YouTuber, that's great—you will have two to three hours on the weekend to practice that, after you have completed all of your tasks and played outside for two to three hours as well.

Also, I hear from a number of parents that their child wants to become a "coder." I'm sorry, but you do not become a coder simply by playing video games that someone else coded. Coding isn't playing; it's serious work that requires serious math skills. Sure, most coders are gamers and enjoy playing, but becoming a coder usually requires countless hours of practice to gain that skill, and you're not gaining that specific skill while playing a game. Do you want them to have a successful life after 18? Get them outside, regardless of how many screens are involved in their dream job.

Remember, you control the environment, not the child. If your house looks like an entertainment arcade, your child will act like they are at one.

Delay the smartphone as long as possible. In addition to causing emotional dysregulation and shortened attention spans, excessive screen use hinders the ability of young kids to develop fine and gross motor skills (Webster et al. 2019; Zain et al. 2023). Without these fundamental skills, kids may struggle to run, jump, throw, catch, or even write comfortably.

If nothing else I've said has convinced you of the harm done by screens, then just look at what they do to kids' physical health. That alone should be reason enough:

extended screen time is linked to poor posture, back pain, and repetitive strain injuries that limit physical capability and can lead to lifelong musculoskeletal issues (Warda et al. 2023). Sedentary screen time replaces active play, increasing the risk of cardiovascular disease through factors such as obesity, low HDL cholesterol, insulin resistance, and high blood pressure—even for young children and adolescents (Lissak 2018).

These aren't the kind of problems that kids just "outgrow." Habits and patterns developed early in life can have a direct impact on health risks as an adult (Shrestha and Copenhaver 2015). High blood pressure, obesity, and lack of physical activity are all associated with excessive screen time, and all of them are risk factors for heart disease.

Yes, you can have a TV, audiobooks, a music player, podcasts, and all of the positive screens I listed earlier. But if your child has constant access to video games, YouTube, a tablet, a smartphone, or a computer—you are already fighting a losing battle. Getting them to engage in meaningful conversations with you and go outside and play with peers will be very hard.

We have to fully accept not just what the screens do to their brains but what they take away from them. This is exactly what Jonathan Haidt talks about in his book *The Anxious Generation* (2024). The phone-based childhood has replaced the play-based childhood, and that is what is fueling this youth mental health crisis. To the child and teen brain, screens are better than everything else. Literally everything. The desire to be a child, make real friendships, and do new things becomes obsolete once screens are introduced.

To make matters even worse, so many parents are addicted too. Avoid constantly scrolling in front of your child. That would be horrible modeling of behavior, and it would send a message to your child that the phone is more interesting than they are. We cannot allow ADHD kids who already struggle with self-image to think that for a millisecond.

What makes me so passionate about this topic is that screens do not allow ADHD kids to discover their talents. ADHD kids are capable of anything. I never underestimate them and their abilities to overcome the odds and exceed expectations. However, when their entire childhood is spent in the virtual world, their talents and skills stay within and never see the daylight. They sit dormant forever.

That child with ADHD who you thought was completely unathletic and not interested in sports could be an incredible athlete who benefits greatly from constant exercise and teammate bonding. But you never got to find out because you thought screens were "social" and kids didn't play outside anymore, and you didn't want your child to feel left out. Maybe that child with ADHD is an amazing artist, musician, writer, public speaker, designer, but we never got to find out because you gave them video games so they could play online with peers and feel included. Screens make dreams and talents die.

I have worked with so many families that did the hard thing. They removed the screens, persevered through the behaviors, and created a new and beneficial structure at home. They watched as their kids became more regulated, slept better at night, and ate healthier foods. Their child became more social, spending hours after school outside riding bikes, going to friends' houses, joining after-school clubs and activities, and finding new interests and talents. Their child became more independent with morning routines, homework, and evening routines.

Every single one of them, and I mean it—every single one of them, with 100% accuracy—saw positive progress from their child. In all my years of working with families to eliminate screens for their ADHD child or teen, not a single one has ever regretted it.

However, none of them enjoyed the process. Those few weeks of withdrawal were hard. If you remove screens, you are going to experience extreme dysregulation and behaviors. We have to accept that these reactions are inevitable. If you have ever watched the show *Intervention*, you know what it's like to remove an addicting substance from an addict. If it was easy and peaceful, they wouldn't have a show.

Just remind yourself as much as possible—the withdrawals will not last.

A family has never come back to me and said, "Oh my goodness, why did I do that? It just made things worse!" Here is what I typically hear from parents after they successfully removed screens and persevered through all of the withdrawal behaviors:

> "I am just upset I didn't do this sooner!"
>
> "I always knew deep down that I needed to do this, I just needed someone to tell me to do it and give me the strength."
>
> "Those first two weeks were rough! He did everything he could to make us change our mind, but we stayed strong and didn't budge, and boy am I glad I did!"
>
> "I feel like I have my son back! He actually talks to me now. I actually know what is happening at school, who his friends are, and how he feels about things."
>
> "She will actually come sit with us at dinner now and talk to us. We haven't done that in years."

Yes, parents, it is incredibly scary, but you can do this.

Free-Range Kids

Play—true outdoor, unstructured play—is the most important thing for children from birth to 18 years old. This is truly where executive functions and social skills are developed (Rosiek et al. 2022; Koepp et al. 2022; Lee et al. 2020)—outside, away from parents, away from adults, with peers, learning cause and effect and social reciprocity through play.

Many of you reading this book can clearly remember a time when you would go outside to play with friends for hours every day after school. You only knew to come home when the streetlights would come on. You had no phone or GPS to help you get home; you had to figure it out yourself. It was a time when all the kids in the neighborhood got together to ride bikes, play sports, and enjoy the outdoors regardless of how much they had in common.

There is no generation of youth that needs that type of lifestyle more than today's kids. But sadly, this idea has become taboo. We live in a country now where it is too crazy of an idea to let your kids go play outside independently without adult supervision. In some states, you could even get arrested for doing this.

Kids were not designed to sit in a house all day after school, and this is absolutely inhibiting the development of executive function skills. Their bodies were designed to move, explore, climb, run, fall down, and get back up.

When a child stays within the walls of the home all day, they are under their parents' microscope far too often. This negative trend is creating unintentional helicopter parents. It is not their fault—the child just happens to be home all of the time. The messes they create, the noise they make, all the unhealthy snacks they eat, and the constant pestering of siblings is all far too noticeable. Being at home is a recipe for disaster.

There are many things to blame for this. Of course screens are the number-one culprit. But we also have the 24-hour news cycle and social media, scaring parents into believing in "stranger danger," which is massively overblown. We don't focus on facts and reality anymore. With the rise of social media, it's only about emotion, which requires no evidence. Today's outside world has never been safer for kids. There is a greater probability of them getting struck by lightning multiple times than encountering a kidnapper. All the criminals are on the Internet now, trying to trick children on Minecraft, Roblox, Fortnite, Snapchat, Instagram. The virtual world is unfiltered, unchecked, and terrifying when you look at the raw data.

Homework is another culprit. After sitting at an uncomfortable desk all day at school, where there is ever-declining recess time, this child now needs to move and play and be in nature. This is the parents' responsibility as well, to ensure that any time regained from homework isn't just used for screens and being sedentary. If teachers play their role in decreasing homework and following the research, the parents need to do the same.

As Lenore Skenazy, co-founder of Let Grow, states, we need "free range" kids (Skenazy 2008). Lenore was dubbed "the worst mom ever" when she let her nine-year-old son ride the New York City subway by himself, after he stated that it was something personal to him that he wanted to do. Her decision created a media firestorm and a contentious discussion about what we should let kids do without adult supervision.

Ever since, Lenore has devoted her life to spreading information and resources to families who also want to help their children develop independence, based on research—not fear. Along with Peter Gray, Daniel Shuchman, and Jonathan

Haidt, she helped launch the great Let Grow organization, which partners with schools to help create unstructured play groups for students after school (Let Grow 2025). It has been an overwhelming success, and more schools need to be aware of their work and bring them in.

LetGrow isn't the only group promoting this idea. Parents, do some research and learn about the other amazing organizations that are preaching this same message, including 1,000 Hours Outside and TimberNook. Like me, they are not afraid to speak the truth, no matter how hard or annoying it is to hear.

Final Strategies for Teachers: Project-Based Learning

The "lecture-listen" model of American education is insanely outdated. It is simply not how we learn, and definitely not how our youth learns, with their slowly developing brains.

There are ways to cover the material in the curriculum while also increasing student engagement and participation. One method for this is project-based learning.

There is a mountain of evidence showing the positive effects of this method of learning on overall student engagement as well as information retention (Firdausih and Aslan 2024; Zhang and Ma 2023; Krajcik et al. 2023). Here are some specific examples of project-based learning that provide opportunities for students to use their creativity and strengthen their executive functions:

- ♦ Elementary students can learn about ecosystems and insects by designing and constructing a "bug hotel" using natural materials. Have them research which insects will benefit from their "hotel" and present their findings.

- A classroom garden is a great way for young kids to explore plant life cycles and sustainability. Have students grow a mini garden, track plant growth in journals, and learn about healthy eating by planning recipes that use their harvest.
- As kids move onto middle school, the projects can become more elaborate. You can ask students to create a 3D model of a futuristic, sustainable "eco-city" using recycled materials. Depending on the grade level, students can be challenged to address urban issues like pollution and overcrowding.
- History class often relies on the "lecture-listen" model, but it doesn't have to. Ask students to research a historical figure or event and then present their findings in a creative format. This could be a play, a mock trial, or a documentary.
- By the high school level, there are even more options. For example, students can develop communication and technical skills by creating a podcast series about a subject that's important to them. They can incorporate interviews, research, and storytelling to raise awareness about their topic.
- Another great project is an "Escape Room Challenge." Here, students will need to use critical thinking and collaboration skills in order to design an educational escape room for their peers. The "escape route" will be based on material they've learned (like solving math puzzles or answering questions about a period in history).
- To help students learn about social responsibility as well as business, have them start a business for a cause. This could be a bake sale, a craft shop, or something else. Students can be in charge of all aspects of the business, including finances and marketing, and then donate proceeds to a local charity.

- Some projects work well for all age groups. You can host a Cultural Celebration Day that encourages students to explore diversity and gain global awareness. Have each student research a country or culture, and then do a presentation with food, art, or a performance to share with the class.
- Students can expand their creative and collaborative skills through a school-wide art installation. The kids can come up with their own individual ideas, or they can work together to represent a theme like "Our Futures" or "Building Our Community."
- A good science-oriented project is "Weather Watchers," where students can learn about natural science and data analysis at a grade-appropriate level. Ask students to track weather patterns, create graphs, and present on how weather affects daily life in their own local region.

What all of these projects have in common is that they allow students to be active participants in their own learning. And the more excited and emotionally engaged students are in the classroom, the easier they will find it to develop skills like self-regulation, self-motivation, and self-evaluation.

Final Strategies for Parents: Routines That Work

Parents, wouldn't it be nice to escape the argument vortex for good?

To do this, start by creating a visual timeline using real-world photos of your child doing various tasks of their morning routine. Get a picture of them brushing their teeth, fully dressed in their school clothes, and grabbing their backpack, lunch, and water bottle. This is the key: you need to use that visual timeline to replace all verbal prompting. Remember, verbal prompts are dysregulating to them and feed into the negative behaviors.

Wait by the door or in the car for your child, depending on whether they take the bus or you drive them. You have to stay away from them—no hovering! They want the cat-and-mouse game, but you are not going to give it to them!

If they are late to school, there must be consequences at school. They have to sign in late and explain why they were late. Every two to three late arrivals is an after-school detention.

If you are a parent who needs to get to work on time in the morning and your child causes you to be late, you have several options. You can explain to your job that you are trying out a new parenting strategy, and you may be late during this time. Of course, not every job will allow this. If you have the resources, you can hire a college student or another individual to take over morning drop-offs from you. You can contact another parent in your community or district and arrange a carpool for both kids. The social aspect of having a peer rely on your child to get to school on time will be very helpful to them.

When your child comes home after school, remember: homework should be done away from the home and away from parents. It is too tempting to seek negative attention with the unconditional love of parents present. It is also too distracting to do homework in the home, where they look to relax. Homework should be done at school, at the local library, with a classmate, or supervised by a college student, tutor, or other educational staff.

Any time homework is not explicitly being worked on, the school laptop should be in the parents' possession. The school laptop should never go into the child's bedroom. We don't want them to ever use that for entertainment purposes.

The evening routine should follow a similar format as the morning routine. Again, create the visual timeline of steps to be completed. One thing to keep in mind here: we have to get out of the habit of forcing our kids to follow a routine to get to sleep at a specific time. This causes the parent to ferociously follow the child around to ensure they are doing everything correctly and in a timely manner. This is exactly what the ADHD brain wants—constant attention. When you do this, you are making it more stimulating to do the wrong thing instead of doing the right thing and getting only a quick sentence of praise.

Instead, set the expectation that they must be in their room at a specific time. Inside their room, they can have access to books and specific toys like LEGOs. Don't pressure them into actually going to sleep—that will cause too much anxiety. Make it more about "winding down," and ensure they are simply in their room and not getting out. They can do whatever they want in their room once they are in there alone. Of course, you, the parent, have full control over what they have access to in their room.

When bedtime rolls around, you are not going to talk your child into going to bed—you are going to *show them*. Bedtime needs to be a family routine. If they think they are going to bed while you get to stay up and watch Netflix, they will interpret that as a massive injustice. You need to show them that you are going to bed too, and all the steps you take to make that happen. They don't have to know that you are actually going to lie in bed and watch things on your phone or the bedroom TV. You're the adult—you're allowed to do that. We just need the kids to think you're going to bed too.

Finally, no screens at least three hours before bedtime. Zero tolerance, that's the rule. No phones or electronics in the bedroom with them. Period. We've seen the research to back this up (Staples et al. 2021; Lissak 2018; Hale and Guan 2015); it's just hard to implement and follow.

But you are the parent and you have to do it, even if they complain. Make sure the Wi-Fi is completely off. Unplug the router and hide it. Utilize white noise, brown noise, or other sound machines to help calm their minds.

By making these changes in your household, you give your kids the opportunity to develop the self-awareness, self-regulation, self-motivation, and self-evaluation they need to thrive.

ADHD Hope for All of Us

Any child with ADHD can develop executive functions. But it is not going to happen unless we fully believe in our children. We have to believe that our children are good and capable. We have to set the bar high for them and hold them to a high standard. When you do that consistently, with love and limits, your child will achieve things thought you could only dream of. This is the definition of ADHD hope, and this is the message you need to come away with from this book—your child with ADHD is capable of anything. They can achieve their dreams and live a greater life than we did before them.

Thank you for taking the time to make this book a part of your life. I hope I get to meet you someday.

—Mike

To learn about the services that GrowNOW provides please visit GrowNOWADHD.com and follow on Instagram @GrowNOWADHD.

Acknowledgments

I want to thank the Jossey-Bass team at Wiley for partnering with me along this writing journey.

With an absolutely full heart and a tear in my eye, I want to thank the entire GrowNOW team. Aside from being able to help others, having you all in my life is the greatest blessing of this work. To even be associated with you all and to call so many of you my friends, colleagues, and co-workers means more to me than I can express with words. This work would not be nearly as meaningful if I didn't get to do it alongside all of you. I have the absolute deepest love and affection for each and every one of you. You all keep me going in more ways than you could ever imagine.

I would also like to thank a friend who helped me edit my writing and coach me to stay on course, Eleri Denham. Eleri was such a privilege to work with, and she gave me the confidence to keep writing.

Of course, this book would not be possible without the support of my beautiful wife Laura, who watched me sit on my phone and computer and type away for hours and hours when I probably should have organized my day and time much better. Thank you for all the support, I love you. Also, my mom and dad—the greatest parents in the world. From the moment I was born, both my mom and dad stopped focusing on themselves and lived only for me and my brother. Everything they did, they did for us. I couldn't ask for better or more loving parents. Thank you for everything, I love you both.

There is one person on this earth who is the meaning for every single thing I do, every breath I take, and every smile and laugh that comes across my face. My daughter Eden is my life's greatest blessing. Her arrival and the start of her life helped me make sense of mine. The joy, happiness, and peace she brings every second of my days is unfathomable. Eden, being your dad is the greatest gift I have ever received. You are my best friend, and I will be there for you forever and always. I love you so much.

References

ADHD Videos (2014a). *The Neuroanatomy of ADHD and thus how to treat ADHD – CADDAC – Dr Russel [sic] Barkley part 3ALL.* September 2. Available at: https://www.youtube.com/watch?v=sPFmKu2S5XY&list=PLzBixSjmbc8cGW9p3-elS6uDHv7T0Z2vp (accessed: November 7, 2024).

ADHD Videos (2014b). *The Neuroanatomy of ADHD and thus how to treat ADHD – CADDAC – Dr Russel [sic] Barkley part 3ALL.* September 2. Available at: https://www.youtube.com/watch?v=sPFmKu2S5XY&list=PLzBixSjmbc8cGW9p3-elS6uDHv7T0Z2vp (accessed: November 7, 2024).

ADHD Videos (2014c). *The Neuroanatomy of ADHD and thus how to treat ADHD – CADDAC – Dr Russel [sic] Barkley part 1ALL.* September 2. Available at: https://www.youtube.com/watch?v=GyZtYzFq4WY (accessed: November 7, 2024).

ADHDtips (2013). *ADHD: Emotional Impulsiveness – Dr. Russell Barkley.* June 16. Available at: https://www.youtube.com/watch?v=VBR_3WKdXJI (accessed: November 22, 2024).

Akbasli, S., Sahin, M., and Yaykiran, Z. (2016). The effect of reading comprehension on the performance in science and mathematics. *Journal of Education and Practice,* 7(16), pp. 108–121.

Al-Quran, M.W.M. (2022). Traditional media versus social media: Challenges and opportunities. *Technium: Romanian Journal of Applied Sciences and Technology,* 4(10), pp. 145–160. https://doi.org/10.47577/technium.v4i10.8012.

Alvarez-Peregrina, C., Sánchez-Tena, M.Á., Martinez-Perez, C., and Villa-Collar, C. (2020). The relationship between screen and outdoor time with rates of myopia in Spanish children. *Frontiers in Public Health, 8.* https://doi.org/10.3389/fpubh.2020.560378.

Amen, D. (2020). Coping with ADHD and trying to notice what you like more than dislike. Interview with Tana Amen, *The Brain Warrior's Way Podcast.* Available at: https://brainwarriorswaypodcast.com/coping-with-adhd-and-trying-to-notice-what-you-like-more-than-dislike/ (accessed: January 5, 2025).

Arnsten, A.F.T. (2009). Toward a new understanding of attention-deficit hyperactivity disorder pathophysiology. *CNS Drugs 23*(Suppl 1), pp. 33–41. https://doi.org/10.2165/00023210.200923000-00005.

Asarnow, L.D. and Mirchandaney, R. (2020). Sleep and mood disorders among youth. *Child and Adolescent Psychiatric Clinics of North America, 30*(1), pp. 251–268. https://doi.org/10.1016/j.chc.2020.09.003.

Barbaresi, W.J., Katusic, S.K., Colligan, R.C., Weaver, A.L., and Jacobsen, S.J. (2007). Long-term school outcomes for children with attention-deficit/hyperactivity disorder: A population-based perspective. *Journal of Developmental & Behavioral Pediatrics, 28*(4), pp. 265–273. https://doi.org/10.1097/DBP.0b013e31811ff87d.

Barkley, R.A. (2005). *Attention-Deficit Hyperactivity Disorder, Third Edition: A Handbook for Diagnosis and Treatment.* Guilford Publications, USA.

Barkley, R.A. (2015). *Attention-Deficit Hyperactivity Disorder, Fourth Edition: A Handbook for Diagnosis and Treatment.* Guilford Publications, USA.

Barkley, R.A. (2022). *Treating ADHD in Children and Adolescents.* Guilford Publications, USA.

Barkley, R.A. (2023). ADHD: Nature, course, outcomes, and comorbidity. ContinuingEdCourses.Net. Available at: https://www.continuingedcourses.net/active/courses/course082.php.

Barkley, R.A. and Cox, D. (2007). A review of driving risks and impairments associated with attention-deficit/hyperactivity disorder and the effects of stimulant medication on driving performance. *Journal of Safety Research, 38*(1), pp. 113–128. https://doi.org/10.1016/j.jsr.2006.09.004.

Barkley, R.A., Murphy, K.R., and Fischer, M. (2008). *ADHD in Adults: What the Science Says.* Guilford Press, USA.

Baumgartner, S.E., Weeda, W.D., van der Heijden, L.L., and Huizinga, M. (2014). The relationship between media multitasking and executive function in early adolescents. *The Journal of Early Adolescence, 34*(8), pp. 1120–1144. https://doi.org/10.1177/0272431614523133.

Beard, V. (2018). A study of the purpose and value of recess in elementary schools as perceived by teachers and administrators. Doctoral dissertation. East Tennessee State University. Available at: https://dc.etsu.edu/etd/3433 (accessed: January 10, 2025).

Biederman, J., Wilens, T., Mick, E., Milberger, S., Spencer, T.J., and Faraone, S.V. (1995). Psychoactive substance use disorders in adults with attention deficit hyperactivity disorder (ADHD): Effects of ADHD and psychiatric comorbidity. *American Journal of Psychiatry, 152*(11), pp. 1652–1658.

Biederman, J., Mick, E., Faraone, S.V., Braaten, E., Doyle, A., Spencer, T., Wilens, T.E., Frazier, E., and Johnson, M.A. (2002). Influence of gender on attention deficit hyperactivity disorder in children referred to a psychiatric clinic. *American Journal of Psychiatry, 159*(1), pp. 36–42. https://doi.org/10.1176/appi.ajp.159.1.36.

Bočanová, J. (2024). Withdrawal, withdrawal symptoms, and craving in gaming disorder – Systematic review. *Addictology, 24*(1), pp. 49–58. https://doi.org/10.35198/01-2024-001-0002.

Breslau, J., Miller, E., Chung, W.J.J., and Schweitzer, J.B. (2011). Childhood and adolescent onset psychiatric disorders, substance use, and failure to graduate high school on time. *Journal of Psychiatric Research, 45*(3), pp. 295–301.

Brez, C. and Sheets, V. (2017). Classroom benefits of recess. *Learning Environments Research, 20,* pp. 433–445. https://doi.org/10.1007/s10984-017-9237-x.

Bushman, B.J. and Huesmann, L.R. (2006). Short-term and long-term effects of violent media on aggression in children and adults. *Archives of Pediatrics & Adolescent Medicine, 160*(4), pp. 348–352. https://doi.org/10.1001/archpedi.160.4.348.

Carlson, C.L. (2010). Adolescent literacy, dropout factories, and the economy: The relationship between literacy, graduation rates, and economic development in the United States. *Education, 1,* pp. 1–8. Available at: http://jehd.thebrpi.org/journals/jehd/Vol_2_No_1_June_2013/1.pdf (accessed: January 10, 2025).

Chang, D. (2024). Middle schoolers impersonate teachers in lewd, homophobic, racist TikTok videos, officials say. *NBC10 Philadelphia* (July 8). Available at: https://www.nbcphiladelphia.com/news/local/middle-schoolers-impersonate-teachers-in-lewd-homophobic-racist-tiktok-videos-officials-say/3905913/ (accessed: January 10, 2025).

Clayton, N.S., Salwiczek, L.H., and Dickinson, A. (2007). Episodic memory. *Current Biology, 17*(6), pp. R189–R191. https://doi.org/10.1016/j.cub.2007.01.011.

Clements, R. (2004). An investigation of the status of outdoor play. *Contemporary Issues in Early Childhood, 5*(1), pp. 68–80. https://doi.org/10.2304/ciec.2004.5.1.10.

Cleveland Clinic (2022). Dopamine. ClevelandClinic.org. Available at: https://my.clevelandclinic.org/health/articles/22581-dopamine (accessed: December 11, 2024).

Cole, M., John-Steiner, V., Scribner, S., and Souberman, E. (eds.) (1978). *Mind in Society: The Development of Higher Psychological Processes.* L.S. Vygotsky. Harvard University Press, USA.

Danielson, M.L., Bitsko, R.H., Ghandour, R.M., Holbrook, J.R., Kogan, M.D., and Blumberg, S.J. (2018). Prevalence of parent-reported ADHD diagnosis and associated treatment among US children and adolescents, 2016. *Journal of Clinical Child & Adolescent Psychology, 47*(2), pp. 199–212. https://doi.org/10.1080/15374416.2017.1417860.

Danielson, M.L., Claussen, A.H., Bitsko, R.H., Katz, S.M., Newsome, K., Blumberg, S.J., Kogan, M.D., and Ghandour, R. (2024). ADHD prevalence among U.S. children and adolescents in 2022: Diagnosis, severity, co-occurring disorders, and treatment. *Journal of Clinical Child & Adolescent Psychology, 53*(3), pp. 343–360. https://doi.org/10.1080/15374416.2024.2335625.

Ding, K., Shen, Y., Liu, Q., and Li, H. (2023). The effects of digital addiction on brain function and structure of children and adolescents: A scoping review. *Healthcare, 12*(1), p. 15. https://doi.org/10.3390/healthcare12010015.

DuPaul, G.J., Kern, L., Caskie, G.I., and Volpe, R.J. (2015). Early intervention for young children with attention deficit hyperactivity disorder: Prediction of academic and behavioral outcomes. *School Psychology Review, 44*(1), pp. 3–20.

DuPaul, G.J., Morgan, P.L., Farkas, G., Hillemeier, M.M., and Maczuga, S. (2018). Eight-year latent class trajectories of academic and social functioning in children with attention-deficit/hyperactivity disorder. *Journal of*

Abnormal Child Psychology, 46, pp. 979–992. https://doi.org/10.1007/s10802-017-0344-z.

EdTech Evidence Exchange (2021). Overview: U.S. K-12 public education technology spending. University of Virginia. Available at: FINAL K12 EdTech Funding Analysis_v.1 (accessed: December 30, 2024).

Faraone, S.V. (2015). Attention deficit hyperactivity disorder and premature death. *The Lancet, 385*(9983), pp. 2132–2133. https://doi.org/10.1016/S0140-6736(14)61822-5.

Faraone, S.V., Perlis, R.H., Doyle, A.E., Smoller, J.W., Goralnick, J.J., Holmgren, M.A., and Sklar, P. (2005). Molecular genetics of attention-deficit/hyperactivity disorder. *Biological Psychiatry, 57*(11), pp. 1313–1323.

Firdausih, F. and Aslan, A. (2024). Literature review: The effect of project-based learning on student motivation and achievement in science. *Indonesian Journal of Education, 4*(3), pp. 1011–1022.

Fuller-Thomson, E., Rivière, R.N., Carrique, L., and Agbeyaka, S. (2020). The dark side of ADHD: Factors associated with suicide attempts among those with ADHD in a national representative Canadian sample. *Archives of Suicide Research, 26*(3), pp. 1122–1140. https://doi.org/10.1080/13811118.2020.1856258.

George, A.S., George, A.H., Baskar, T., and Shahul, A. (2023). Screens steal time: How excessive screen use impacts the lives of young people. *Partners Universal Innovative Research Publication, 1*(2), pp. 157–177. https://doi.org/10.5281/zenodo.10.50536.

Griffiths, M.D. (2018). Adolescent social networking: How do social media operators facilitate habitual use? *Education and Health, 36*(3), pp. 66–69.

Grimm, O., Kranz, T.M., and Reif, A. (2020). Genetics of ADHD: What should the clinician know? *Current Psychiatry Reports, 22,* pp. 1–8. https://doi.org/10.1007/s11920-020-1141-x.

Haghani, M., Abbasi, S., Abdoli, L., Shams, S.F., Zarandi, B.F.B.B., Shokrpour, N., Jahromizadeh, A., Mortazavi, S.A., and Mortazavi, S.M.J. (2024). Blue light and digital screens revisited: A new look at blue light from the vision quality, circadian rhythm and cognitive functions perspective. *Journal of Biomedical Physics & Engineering, 14*(3), p. 213. https://doi.org/10.31661/jbpe.v0i0.2106-1355.

Haidt, J. (2024). *The Anxious Generation: How the Great Rewiring of Childhood Is Causing an Epidemic of Mental Illness*. Penguin Press, USA.

Hale, L. and Guan, S. (2015). Screen time and sleep among school-aged children and adolescents: A systematic literature review. *Sleep Medicine Reviews, 21,* pp. 50–58. https://doi.org/10.1016/j.smrv.2014.07.007.

Hechtman, L., Swanson, J.M., Sibley, M.H., Stehli, A., Owens, E.B., Mitchell, J.T., Arnold, L.E., Molina, B.S., Hinshaw, S.P., Jensen, P.S., and Abikoff, H.B. (2016). Functional adult outcomes 16 years after childhood diagnosis of attention-deficit/hyperactivity disorder: MTA results. *Journal of the American Academy of Child & Adolescent Psychiatry, 55*(11), pp. 945–952. https://doi.org/10.1016/j.jaac.2016.07.774.

Hodges, V.C., Centeio, E.E., and Morgan, C.F. (2022). The benefits of school recess: A systematic review. *Journal of School Health, 92*(10), pp. 959–967. https://doi.org/10.1111/josh.13230.

Howie, E.K., Perryman, K.L., Moretta, J., and Cameron, L. (2023). Educational outcomes of recess in elementary school children: A mixed-methods systematic review. *PLOS ONE, 18*(11). https://doi.org/10.1371/journal.pone.0294340.

Jangmo, A., Kuja-Halkola, R., Pérez-Vigil, A., Almqvist, C., Bulik, C.M., D'Onofrio, B., Lichtenstein, P., Ahnemark, E., Werner-Kiechle, T., and Larsson, H. (2021).

Attention-deficit/hyperactivity disorder and occupational outcomes: The role of educational attainment, comorbid developmental disorders, and intellectual disability. *PLOS One, 16*(3). https://doi.org/10.1371/journal.pone.0247724.

Kent, K.M., Pelham Jr, W.E., Molina, B.S., Sibley, M.H., Waschbusch, D.A., Yu, J., Gnagy, E.M., Biswas, A., Babinski, D.E., and Karch, K.M. (2011). The academic experience of male high school students with ADHD. *Journal of Abnormal Child Psychology, 39*(3), pp. 451–462.

Kessler, R.C., Adler, L., Barkley, R., Biederman, J., Conners, C.K., Demler, O., Faraone, S.V., Greenhill, L.L., Howes, M.J., Secnik, K., and Spencer, T. (2006). The prevalence and correlates of adult ADHD in the United States: Results from the National Comorbidity Survey Replication. *American Journal of Psychiatry, 163*(4), pp. 716–723. https://doi.org/10.1176/ajp.2006.163.4.716.

Koepp, A.E., Gershoff, E.T., Castelli, D.M., and Bryan, A.E. (2022). Preschoolers' executive functions following indoor and outdoor free play. *Trends in Neuroscience and Education, 28*, p. 100182. https://doi.org/10.1016/j.tine.2022.10.182.

Kohn, A. (2006). *The Homework Myth: Why Our Kids Get Too Much of a Bad Thing.* Da Capo Books, USA.

Krajcik, J., Schneider, B., Miller, E.A., Chen, I.C., Bradford, L., Baker, Q., Bartz, K., Miller, C., Li, T., Codere, S., and Peek-Brown, D. (2023). Assessing the effect of project-based learning on science learning in elementary schools. *American Educational Research Journal, 60*(1), pp. 70–102. https://doi.org/10.3102/00028312221129247.

Lee, R.L.T., Lane, S., Brown, G., Leung, C., Kwok, S.W.H., and Chan, S.W.C. (2020). Systematic review of the impact of unstructured play interventions to improve young children's physical, social, and emotional well-being. *Nursing & Health Sciences, 22*(2), pp. 184–196. https://doi.org/10.1111/nhs.12732.

Leonard, J. (2024). The cognitive scientist helping kids persist through challenges. Interview by Annie Brookman-Byrne, *BOLD* (September 5). Available at: https://boldscience.org/the-cognitive-scientist-helping-kids-persist-through-challenges (accessed: January 4, 2025).

Leonard, J.A., Duckworth, A.L., Schulz, L.E., and Mackey, A.P. (2021). Leveraging cognitive science to foster children's persistence. *Trends in Cognitive Sciences, 25*(8), pp. 642–644. https://doi.org/10.1016/j.tics.2021.05.005.

Let Grow (2025). About. Available at: https://letgrow.org/about-us/ (accessed: January 5, 2025).

Levy, R. (2024). The prefrontal cortex: From monkey to man. *Brain, 147*(3), pp. 794–815. https://doi.org/10.1093/brain/awad389.

Lissak, G. (2018). Adverse physiological and psychological effects of screen time on children and adolescents: Literature review and case study. *Environmental Research, 164*, pp. 149–157. https://doi.org/10.1016/j.envres.2018.01.015.

Liu, J., Riesch, S., Tien, J., Lipman, T., Pinto-Martin, J., and O'Sullivan, A. (2022). Screen media overuse and associated physical, cognitive, and emotional/behavioral outcomes in children and adolescents: An integrative review. *Journal of Pediatric Health Care, 36*(2), pp. 99–109.

Low, F., Gluckman, P., and Poulton, R. (2021). Executive functions: A crucial but overlooked factor for lifelong wellbeing. Koi Tū: The Centre for Informed Futures. Available at: https://informedfutures.org/wp-content/uploads/pdf/Executive-functions-a-crucial-but-overlooked-factor-for-lifelong-wellbeing.pdf (accessed: January 10, 2025).

Madigan, S., McArthur, B.A., Anhorn, C., Eirich, R., and Christakis, D.A. (2020). Associations between screen use and child language skills: A systematic review and meta-analysis. *JAMA Pediatrics, 174*(7), pp. 665–675. https://doi.org/10.1001/jamapediatrics.2020.0327.

Martin, C.A., Papadopoulos, N., Chellew, T., Rinehart, N.J., and Sciberras, E. (2019). Associations between parenting stress, parent mental health and child sleep problems for children with ADHD and ASD: Systematic review. *Research in Developmental Disabilities, 93*, 103463. https://doi.org/10.1016/j.ridd.2019.103463.

Matthews, D. (2017). Logical consequences: Helping kids learn from their mistakes. *Psychology Today* (October 3). Available at: https://www.psychologytoday.com/us/blog/going-beyond-intelligence/201710/logical-consequences-helping-kids-learn-their-mistakes (accessed: January 9, 2025).

McArthur, B.A., Browne, D., Tough, S., and Madigan, S. (2020). Trajectories of screen use during early childhood: Predictors and associated behavior and learning outcomes. *Computers in Human Behavior, 113*. https://doi.org/10.1016/j.chb.2020.106501.

Michielsen, M., De Kruif, J.T.C., Comijs, H.C., Van Mierlo, S., Semeijn, E.J., Beekman, A.T., Deeg, D.J., and Kooij, J.S. (2018). The burden of ADHD in older adults: A qualitative study. *Journal of Attention Disorders, 22*(6), pp. 591–600. https://doi.org/10.1177/1087054715610001.

Mohr-Jensen, C. and Steinhausen, H.C. (2016). A meta-analysis and systematic review of the risks associated with childhood attention-deficit hyperactivity disorder on long-term outcome of arrests, convictions, and incarcerations. *Clinical Psychology Review, 48*, pp. 32–42. https://doi.org/10.1016/j.cpr.2016.05.002.

Montejano, L., Sasané, R., Hodgkins, P., Russo, L., and Huse, D. (2011). Adult ADHD: Prevalence of diagnosis in a US population with employer health insurance. *Current Medical Research and Opinion, 27*(Suppl 2), pp. 5–11. https://doi.org/10.1185/03007995.2011.603302.

Mueller, P.A. and Oppenheimer, D.M. (2014). The pen is mightier than the keyboard: Advantages of longhand over laptop note taking. *Psychological Science, 25*(6), pp. 1159–1168. https://doi.org/10.1177/0956797614524581.

Mullan, K. (2019). A child's day: Trends in time use in the UK from 1975 to 2015. *The British Journal of Sociology, 70*(3), pp. 997–1024. https://doi.org/10.1111/1468-4446.12369.

Mumphrey, C. (2023). ACT test scores for US students drop to new 30-year low. *AP News* (October 11). Available at: https://apnews.com/article/act-college-admission-test-score-optional-99f80b26696a92c78e2680873a3df68c (accessed: December 30, 2024).

Muppalla, S.K., Vuppalapati, S., Pulliahgaru, A.R., and Sreenivasulu, H. (2023). Effects of excessive screen time on child development: An updated review and strategies for management. *Cureus, 15*(6), p. e40608. https://doi.org/10.7759/cureus.40608.

National Center for Education Statistics (2024). U.S. adults score on par with international average in literacy skills, below international average in numeracy and problem-solving skills in survey of adult skills. Available at: https://nces.ed.gov/whatsnew/press_releases/12_10_2024.asp (accessed: January 10, 2025).

National Center for Health Statistics (2023). QuickStats: Percentage of children and adolescents aged 5–17 years who took medication for their mental health or received counseling or therapy from a mental health professional during the past 12 months, by year – National

Health Interview Survey, United States, 2019 and 2022. *Morbidity and Mortality Weekly Report, 72*(43), p. 1171. http://dx.doi.org/10.15585/mmwr.mm7243a5.

O'Rourke, S., Whalley, H., Janes, S., MacSweeney, N., Skrenes, A., Crowson, S., MacLean, L., and Schwannauer, M. (2020). The development of cognitive and emotional maturity in adolescents and its relevance in judicial contexts. Scottish Sentencing Council. Available at: https://www.scottishsentencingcouncil.org.uk/media/mi0aavav/20200219-ssc-cognitive-maturity-literature-review.pdf (accessed: January 10, 2025).

Olfson, M., Druss, B.G., and Marcus, S.C. (2015). Trends in mental health care among children and adolescents. *New England Journal of Medicine, 372*(21), pp. 2029–2038. https://doi.org/10.1056/NEJMsa1413512.

Ozensoy, A.U. (2021). The effect of critical reading skill on academic success in social studies. *Eurasian Journal of Educational Research, 93,* pp. 319–337.

Pagani, L.S., Fitzpatrick, C., Barnett, T.A., and Dubow, E. (2010). Prospective associations between early childhood television exposure and academic, psychosocial, and physical well-being by middle childhood. *Archives of Pediatrics & Adolescent Medicine, 164*(5), pp. 425–431. https://doi.org/10.1001/archpediatrics.2010.50.

Pelham, W.E. III, Page, T.F., Altszuler, A.R., Gnagy, E.M., Molina, B.S.G., and Pelham, W.E., Jr. (2020). The long-term financial outcome of children diagnosed with ADHD. *Journal of Consulting and Clinical Psychology, 88*(2), pp. 160–171. https://doi.org/10.1037/ccp0000461.

Polanczyk, G., de Lima, M.S., Horta, B.L., Biederman, J., and Rohde, L.A. (2007). The worldwide prevalence of ADHD: A systematic review and metaregression analysis. *American Journal of Psychiatry, 164*(6), pp. 942–948. https://doi.org/10.1176/ajp.2007.164.6.942.

Presta, V., Guarnieri, A., Laurenti, F., Mazzei, S., Arcari, M.L., Mirandola, P., Vitale, M., Chia, M.Y.H., Condello, G., and Gobbi, G. (2024). The impact of digital devices on children's health: A systematic literature review. *Journal of Functional Morphology and Kinesiology, 9*(4), p. 236. https://doi.org/10.3390/jfmk9040236.

Qayyum, A., Kashif, M.F., and Shahid, R. (2024). The effect of excessive smartphone use on child cognitive development and academic achievement: A mixed method analysis. *Annals of Human and Social Sciences, 5*(3), pp. 166–181. https://doi.org/10.35484/ahss.2024(5-III)16.

Ragan, E.D., Jennings, S.R., Massey, J.D., and Doolittle, P.E. (2014). Unregulated use of laptops over time in large lecture classes. *Computers & Education, 78*, pp. 78–86. https://doi.org/10.1016/j.compedu.2014.05.002.

Richardson, B., Fife, P.T., Steed, J.D., Crane, C., and Gaskin, J. (2024). The new marshmallow: The effects of screen use on children's ability to delay gratification. *ECIS 2024 Proceedings, 2*.

Rieber, R.W. and Carton, A.S. (eds.) (1987). *The Collected Works of L.S. Vygotsky, Volume 1: Problems of General Psychology*. Plenum Press, USA.

Rizzolatti, G. and Sinigaglia, C. (2016). The mirror mechanism: A basic principle of brain function. *Nature Reviews Neuroscience, 17*(12), pp. 757–765. https://doi.org/10.1038/nrn.2016.135.

Rosiek, M.A., Etnier, J.L., and Willoughby, M.T. (2022). A comparison of the effects of outdoor physical activity and indoor classroom-based activities on measures of executive function in preschoolers. *International Journal of Early Childhood, 54*(2), pp. 203–215. https://doi.org/10.1007/s13158-022-00318-x.

Shrestha, R. and Copenhaver, M. (2015). Long-term effects of childhood risk factors on cardiovascular health during adulthood. *Clinical Medicine Reviews in Vascular Health, 7*, pp. 1–5. https://doi.org/10.4137/CMRVH.S29964.

Singer, D.G., Singer, J.L., D'Agnostino, H., and DeLong, R. (2009). Children's pastimes and play in sixteen nations: Is free-play declining? *American Journal of Play, 1*(3), pp. 283–312.

Skenazy, L. (2008). Why FreeRange? Free-Range Kids. Available at: https://www.freerangekids.com/about/ (accessed: January 5, 2025).

Song, P., Zha, M., Yang, Q., Zhang, Y., Li, X., and Rudan, I. (2021). The prevalence of adult attention-deficit hyperactivity disorder: A global systematic review and meta-analysis. *Journal of Global Health, 11*. https://doi.org/10.7189/jogh.11.04009.

Sriram, K. (2023). To what extent does social media usage impact the ability to delay gratification and attention span of teenagers in Mumbai? *British Journal of Multidisciplinary and Advanced Studies, 4*(6), pp. 71–86. https://doi.org/10.37745/bjmas.2022.0363.

Staples, A.D., Hoyniak, C., McQuillan, M.E., Molfese, V., and Bates, J.E. (2021). Screen use before bedtime: Consequences for nighttime sleep in young children. *Infant Behavior and Development, 62*, p. 101522. https://doi.org/10.1016/j.infbeh.2020.101522.

Stapp, A.C. and Karr, J.K. (2018). Effect of recess on fifth grade students' time on-task in an elementary classroom. *International Electronic Journal of Elementary Education, 10*(4), pp. 449–456. https://doi.org/10.26822/iejee.2018438135.

Stuss, D.T. and Knight, R.T. (eds.) (2013). *Principles of Frontal Lobe Function*. Oxford University Press, USA.

Thomas, R., Sanders, S., Doust, J., Beller, E., and Glasziou, P. (2015). Prevalence of attention-deficit/hyperactivity disorder: A systematic review and meta-analysis. *Pediatrics, 135*(4), pp. e994–e1001. https://doi.org/10.1542/peds.2014-3482.

UNESCO (2023). Global Education Monitoring Report 2023: Technology in education – A tool on whose terms? UNESCO, Paris. https://doi.org/10.54676/UZQV8501.

Volkow, N.D., Wang, G.J., Newcorn, J.H., Kollins, S.H., Wigal, T.L., Telang, F., Fowler, J.S., Goldstein, R.Z., Klein, N., Logan, J., and Wong, C. (2011). Motivation deficit in ADHD is associated with dysfunction of the dopamine reward pathway. *Molecular Psychiatry, 16*(11), pp. 1147–1154. https://doi.org/10.1038/mp.2010.97.

Ward, S. and Jacobsen, K. (2014). Staying a beat ahead. CHADD. Available at: https://chadd.org/wp-content/uploads/2018/06/ATTN_08_14_StayingBeatAhead.pdf (accessed: January 12, 2025).

Warda, D.G., Nwakibu, U., and Nourbakhsh, A. (2023). Neck and upper extremity musculoskeletal symptoms secondary to maladaptive postures caused by cell phones and backpacks in school-aged children and adolescents. *Healthcare, 11*(6), p. 819. https://doi.org/10.3390/healthcare11060819.

Webster, E.K., Martin, C.K., and Staiano, A.E. (2019). Fundamental motor skills, screen-time, and physical activity in preschoolers. *Journal of Sport and Health Science, 8*(2), pp. 114–121. https://doi.org/10.1016/j.jshs.2018.11.006.

Werling, A.M., Kuzhippallil, S., Emery, S., Walitza, S., and Drechsler, R. (2022). Problematic use of digital media in children and adolescents with a diagnosis of attention-deficit/hyperactivity disorder compared to controls. A meta-analysis. *Journal of Behavioral Addictions, 11*(2), pp. 305–325. https://doi.org/10.1556/2006.2022.00007.

Wexelblatt, R. (2021). Your emotional responses to 'bad' behavior are counterproductive. *ADDitude Magazine*

(November 10). Available at: https://www.additudemag.com/emotional-response-adhd-behavior/ (accessed: January 5, 2025).

Wexelblatt, R. (2025). Scaffolding Better Behavior course. ADHD Dude. Available at: https://www.adhddude.com/scaffolding-better-behavior-preview/ (accessed: January 5, 2025).

Wolraich, M.L., Hagan, J.F., Allan, C., Chan, E., Davison, D., Earls, M., Evans, S.W., Flinn, S.K., Froehlich, T., Frost, J., and Holbrook, J.R. (2019). Clinical practice guideline for the diagnosis, evaluation, and treatment of attention-deficit/hyperactivity disorder in children and adolescents. *Pediatrics, 144*(4), p. e20192528. https://doi.org/10.1542/peds.2019-2528.

Young, S., Moss, D., Sedgwick, O., Fridman, M., and Hodgkins, P. (2015). A meta-analysis of the prevalence of attention deficit hyperactivity disorder in incarcerated populations. *Psychological Medicine, 45*(2), pp. 247–258. https://doi.org/10.1017/S0033291714000762.

Zain, N.A.Z.M., Poot, E.F.M., Daud, A.Z.C., Azman, N.A., and Zainudin, A.F. (2023). Correlation between screen time age exposure and screen time duration with developmental skills among children aged 6–36 months: A cross-sectional study. *Journal of Health and Translational Medicine, 2,* pp. 79–85. https://doi.org/10.22452/jummec.sp2023no2.9.

Zastrow, M. (2017). Is video game addiction really an addiction? *Proceedings of the National Academy of Sciences, 114*(17), pp. 4268–4272. https://doi.org/10.1073/pnas.1705077114.

Zhang, L. and Ma, Y. (2023). A study of the impact of project-based learning on student learning effects: A meta-analysis study. *Frontiers in Psychology, 14.* https://doi.org/10.3389/fpsyg.2023.1202728.

Index

A
academics, 21, 108–111
accommodations, children with ADHD, 158
ADHD (attention-deficit hyperactivity disorder)
  diagnosis, 8
  executive functions, 26, 34, 92, 99, 130, 142, 144
  ADHD and, 33
  in girls vs. boys, diagnosis, 8
  heritability of, 10
  impact on job performance and wages, 10
  and life expectancy, 10
  parenting paradox, 94
  prevalence, 7–8
  and relationships, 9
  and school, 8–9
  substance abuse, 9–10
  suicide attempt rate, 10
adolescence with ADHD
  driving and, 9
  education, 9
  and sedentary screen time, 169
  suicide attempt rate, 10
  verbal working memory during, 29
after-school homework routine, 94
aggression, 73, 78, 149
American Academy of Pediatrics, 4
American Sign Language (ASL) interpreter, 158
anxiety, 9, 64, 78, 79, 83, 95, 120, 159, 178
arguments over limits, 72
autobiographical memory, 20

B
Barkley, Russell, 3, 12, 17, 18, 23, 26, 32, 34, 49, 67, 73, 75
Barkley-Vygotsky Model, 30–35
bedtime routine, 46, 94, 178
behavior, 12
  disruptive, 8
  external, 35
  of families, 14
  impulsive, 25, 30, 62

behavior (*continued*)
  negative, 96
  reinforcement, 160
  withdrawal, 115
behavior-based
    disorder, 13, 73
birthday party, 20, 47
boredom, 54, 61, 83, 91,
    107, 108, 144
brain
  ADHD, 45, 93, 96
  conflict-seeking, 121
  detox, 98
  developmental delay, 12
  prefrontal cortex,
    6, 8, 12, 15
  during stressful situation, 84
brain coach, 30, 57, 87
brushing, 119, 177
bullying, 19, 78, 80

C

cause-and-effect thinking,
    36, 39, 155, 158
children with ADHD, 16
  accommodations, 158
  apraxia of speech, 3
  on education, 8
  emotional regulation
    skills, 88
  emotional stability, 79
  environment at home, 10
  executive function delay,
    84

executive function skills, 11
foresight, 62
gender ratio, 8
gratification delay, 37
and GrowNOW, 4
hindsight, 46
homework, 111, 120
internal speech, 29
and LetGrow, 174
masking idea, 112–113
moving beyond
    comfort zone, 147
nonverbal working memory
    during, 16, 39, 108
overuse of screens, 165
parents, 7
personal laptop, 98
prevalence, 7
screens and executive
    functioning, 50
self-awareness, 45
self-evaluation, 152
self-monitoring, 55
self-motivation, 117, 134
self-regulation
    and, 76–77, 85
short time horizon, 48
skill-building, 67
skill development in, 32
in social settings, 62
teachers, 7
time blindness, 65
timeline of process of
    speech, 32–33

Index

verbal working memory during, 16, 29, 39
classroom accommodations, 160, 161
coaching model, 5
cognitive development, 30
comfort zone, 147–151
conditional thinking, 36–39, 62, 65, 84, 117, 155
cyberbullying, 80

D

daily routines, 28, 44, 49, 65, 117
dancing, 20, 99
Dawson, Peg, 3
dependent child, 20
depression, 10, 79, 166
destruction of property, 73
digital addiction, 53
digital dependency, 143
digital media, 53
dopamine, 51, 53, 78, 93, 129
dysregulation, 77, 166, 168

E

education, 19, 20
  ADHD impact on, 8
  adult model of, 4
  app, 132

emotions, 18–19, 21, 26, 83–89
  negative, 113
  and nonverbal working memory, 18–19
  positive, 85
episodic memory, 20–21
  defined, 20
  and self-awareness, 21
evening routine, 35, 171, 178
evidence-based strategies, 161
  for parents, 97
executive age, 12
exercises, 58

F

Focus Foundation, 3
foresight, 22–24
  children with ADHD, 62
  nonverbal working memory, 22–23, 117, 129
free-range kids, 172
frustration, 64, 79, 83, 85, 120
  tolerance, 123

G

gaming, 78, 113
goals, 26
gratification, 23, 25, 99
  delay, 29, 35
  instant, 99, 106–108

GrowNOW, 4–5, 106
  of internal skills, 60
  model of executive function, 13
guided access, nonverbal students, 132

H
habits and patterns, 169
harmony, skills in, 35–36
hindsight, 20, 22, 24
  children with ADHD, 46
home, 112
  environment, 22
  problem at, 71
  screens and executive functioning, 50
  self-awareness at, 44
  self-regulation, 74
homework, 25, 95, 108–111, 120, 173
  after school, 46
  children with ADHD, 111, 120
  meltdowns, 72
hyperactive, 8, 73, 89
hyperfocus, 56

I
"if-then" language, 155, 158
impulsive behavior, 25, 30, 62
inattentive, 8, 73
individual education plans (IEPs), 1
internal dialogue, 28, 29
internalized speech, 28
internal system, 25, 35, 36
irritability, 78

L
language, 2–3, 25, 87
  defined, 2–3
  "if-then," 155
  skills, 109
  vs. speech, 2–3
laptops, at school, 100, 101
lecture-listen model, 31, 174
Let Grow organization, 174
logical consequences, 68
loneliness, 9, 144

M
masking, myth of, 111–115
Mccloskey, George, 3
media multitasking, 53
memory
  negative, 19
  nonverbal working (see nonverbal working memory (NVWM))
  past, 54
  positive, 19, 20

verbal working (*see* verbal working memory (VWM))
working, 53, 67, 128
mirror neurons, 119
mood disorders, 79
morning routine, 30, 35, 46, 65, 178
  battles, 71
  before school, 94
  verbal prompting and warnings, 95

N

negative-attention-stimulation disorder, 93
no filter, phrase, 25
noise-canceling headphones, 126, 127
nonverbal students, guided access, 132
nonverbal working memory (NVWM), 18–20, 22, 25–26
  defined, 16–18
  and emotions, 18–19
  and episodic memory, 20–21
  foresight, 22–23, 117
  as foundational skill, 15, 25
  harmony with, 27
  hindsight, 20, 22–23, 130, 153

P

parents, with ADHD children
  strategies for, 177
  struggle and burnout, 5–6, 108
personal goals, 26, 75
practice, 25, 105, 107
prefrontal cortex, 6, 12, 53
procrastination, 48, 58
project-based learning, 31, 174–177
prompting, 95, 177
  hierarchy, 60
  verbal, 61

R

reading, 108–111, 122–128
  comprehension, 123
real-life activities, 108
recess programs, 90
reciprocal learning, 31
relationships, 43, 49, 92–98

S

school, 19, 21, 23, 25, 159
  homework, 94
  laptops, 100
screen, 63
  addictive and dangerous, 52, 53

screen (*continued*)
and executive functioning, 50–54
final note on, 165–172
limitation, 64
as motivation, 111–115
overuse, 109, 166–167
red flags, 167
screen-free recess, 90
screen use, 109
blue light from, 79
detrimental effects of, 79
gaming, 78
overstimulation from, 79
social media, 78
self-awareness, 2, 21, 27, 53
for ADHD Brain, 45–46
children with ADHD, 45
in classroom, 43–44
with friends, 44–45
lack of, 14, 46
self-defeating comments, 93
self-evaluation, 142, 144
delayed, 152
lack of, 15
self-image, 140
self-improvement, 133–135
self-monitoring, 53
children with ADHD, 55
component of, 55
prompts, 61
self-motivation, 129
lack of, 15, 106
self-reflection, 59, 60

self-regulation, 21, 71, 74, 83, 105, 129
deficit disorder, 72–78
lack of, 14
self-sabotage, 78
self-talk, 19, 54, 75, 92
management, 16
power of, 28–30
senses, 18, 26
short-term memory, 31
siblings, 22, 64, 73, 93, 97, 131, 173
situational awareness, 53
in social settings, 61–64
smell, 18
social experiences, 19, 21–22, 25
social learning, 31
social media, 63, 112
screen use, 78
social skills, 63
speech, 2
internalizing of, 32
outline process of, 33
timeline of, 32
speech-language pathology (SLP), 3
speech therapy, 2
sports, 19, 21, 25
stress, 10, 49, 64, 72, 79, 95, 156, 159
study skills, 128–133
subtypes, ADHD, 73
summer camp, 20–21

T

tantrums, 25, 73, 106
task paralysis, 49, 55, 56, 58
taste, 18
teacher, 31, 56, 76, 111
   classroom tasks, 92
   one-on-one attention, 126
teens with ADHD, 2, 7, 57
   executive functioning, 160
   four pillars, 14
   friendship, 62
   GrowNOW, 4
   NVWM and VWM, 16
   screen use, 78
   self-awareness, 46, 48, 67
   self-monitoring, 55
   self-regulation, 88
   situational awareness, 62
   vs. without ADHD, 38
texting, 18
time blindness, 16, 49, 56, 65
   children with ADHD, 65
time horizon, 47
trauma, 19, 118

V

verbal working memory (VWM), 27–28, 123
   adolescence, 29
   as brain coach, 16
   childhood, 29
   defined, 16
   as foundational skill, 15
video games, 22, 135, 168, 170
vision board, 125, 127
visual imagery system, 16, 19, 26, 54, 108, 123, 125
visual monitoring tools, 61
voice recording, 127
Vygotsky, Lev, 32, 33

W

Ward, Sarah, 3
withdrawal behaviors, 110, 115, 150, 171
working memory
   nonverbal, 18–19, 26, 156
   verbal, 27–28, 123
writing, 65, 108–111, 122–128

Y

YouTube, 24, 110, 133, 135, 168

Z

zero tolerance, 179